Roderick Hunt

Ghosts Witches

and Things like that...

Oxford University Press

Oxford University Press, Walton Street, Oxford OX2 6DP

Oxford New York Toronto
Delhi Bombay Calcutta Madras Karachi
Petaling Jaya Singapore Hong Kong Tokyo
Nairobi Dar es Salaam Cape Town
Melbourne Auckland

and associated companies in
Beirut Berlin Ibadan Nicosia

Oxford is a trade mark of Oxford University Press

This arrangement and selection © Oxford University Press
1984

First published 1984
Reprinted 1986

ISBN 0 19 278108 1

British Library Cataloguing in Publication Data

Hunt, Roderick, 1939–
Ghosts, Witches, and things like that...
1. Halloween
I. Title
394.2'683   GT4965

To Chris, David, John, Joseph, Julian, Llinos, Nerys,
Nikki, Michelle, Rhian, Tina, and Teresa, who enjoy
a good spooky party.

Typeset by Tradespools Ltd, Frome, Somerset
Printed in Hong Kong

Contents

Acknowledgements

The author and publisher wish to thank the following for permission to use extracts from copyright material:

Harry Behn: 'Ghosts' from *The Golden Hive*. Used by permission of Curtis Brown, Ltd. Copyright © 1957, 1962, 1966 by Harry Behn.
R. V. Beaumont: 'Colonel Fazackerley' – musical setting reprinted by permission of R. V. Beaumont.
Charles Causley: 'Colonel Fazackerley' (words) from *Figgie Hobbin* (Macmillan). Reprinted by permission of David Higham Associates, Ltd.
Pauline Clarke: 'All Hallowe'en'. Reprinted by permission of the author.
Daniel Farson: Extract from *Ghosts in Fact and Fiction*. Reprinted by permission of Irene Josephy.
Peter Haining: 'The Witch Stone of Scrapfaggot Green' from *The Screaming Skull*, edited by Peter Haining. Reprinted by permission of Fontana Paperbacks and Euro-Features, Ltd.
Eric James: 'Forbidden Sounds'. Reprinted by permission of the author.
Randall Jarrell: 'The Bird of Night', published in the UK in *The Lost World* (Eyre & Spottiswoode Ltd. 1966), and in the USA in *The Bat-Poet*. Copyright © Macmillan Publishing Company Incorporated, 1963, 1964. Reprinted by permission of Methuen, London and Macmillan Publishing Co. Inc.
John Kitching: 'Hallowe'en', first published in *A Second Poetry Book*, edited by John Foster, (O.U.P., 1980). Reprinted by permission of the author.
Diarmid Macmanus: 'The Coach of Death' adapted from a chapter of the same name in *Between Two Worlds* (Colin Smythe Ltd., 1977). Adapted and reprinted by permission of Colin Smythe Ltd.
Eric Maple: 'Ghosts' from *Old Wives Tales*. Copyright © Eric Maple. Reprinted by permission of the author.
Lilian Moore: 'Witch goes Shopping' from *See my Lovely Poison Ivy*. Text Copyright © by Lilian Moore. Reprinted by permission of Atheneum Publishers, Inc.
Jack Prelutsky: 'The Witch' from *Nightmares*. Copyright © 1976 by Jack Prelutsky. By permission of Greenwillow Books (A division of William Morrow & Co.) and A. & C. Black (Publishers) Ltd.
Sean Richards: 'The Ghost who haunted a Jet' from *Fun to Know about Ghosts*. Reprinted by permission of Fontana Paperbacks and Euro-Features, Ltd.
Ruth Mather Skidmore: 'Fantasy'.
Marie Winn: 'Have you seen the ghost of John?' from *The Fireside Book of Children's Songs*. Copyright © 1966 by Marie Winn & Allan Miller. Reprinted by permission of Simon & Schuster, Inc.

The publishers have made every effort to trace and contact copyright holders, but in some cases without success, and apologize for any infringement of copyright.

The publishers would like to thank the following for their permission to reproduce photographs:

BBC Hulton Picture Library: p.34 (left), 44, 47 (middle), 66; Bilderdienst Süddeutscher Verlag: p.117 (top); Bodleian Library, Oxford: p. 70 (bottom), 72 (top); Bradford Art Gallery and Museums: p.10 (top right); Brotherton Collection/University of Leeds: p.74 (top); Colorific: p. 22, 45 (top right); Mary Evans Picture Library: p.26, 27, 28 (top right), 31, 34 (right), 47 (top and bottom), 48, 49 (left), 50 (top right), 72 (bottom), 74 (bottom right), 75, 80 (left), 82, 88, 100, 103, 105 (left, bottom right), 110; Mary Evans/Andrew Green: p.117 (bottom right); Fortean Picture Library: p.80/81, 102; Ronald Grant: p.81 (right), 89 (bottom left, centre right); Richard and Sally Greenhill: p.121; Hereford City Museums: p. 45 (bottom right); Michael Holford: p.45 (left); Mansell Collection: p.46, 49 (left), 50 (bottom), 51, 67, 70 (top), 71, 73, 104; Royal Commonwealth Society: p.113; Brian Shuel: p.10 (left), 14, 59; Cathy Sprent: p.115; Sussex Archaeological Society/Reeves Collection courtesy of the Sunday Times: p.41; Whitby Museum: p.92; Zeta Picture Library: p.9, 11, 40, 89, 96/97; "Thieves using a Hand of Glory" from Harper: Half-hours with the highwaymen. And the following for their time and assistance: Dr. and Mrs. Martin Francis, Mrs. Brenda Hunt, Dr. E. W. Poole, EEG Department, The Radcliffe Infirmary.

Studio and location photographs by: Nick Fogden, Mark Mason, Terry Williams.

Illustrations by:
Victor Ambrus pp.90–91; **Debbie Cook** pp.21, 23, 25, 32–33, 39, 64–65; **Alan Curless** pp. 7, 43, 69, 77, 99; **Simon Dorrell** pp.134–135; **Nick Harris** pp.54, 55, 57, 129–130; **Colin Hawkins** p.52, 78–79, 86–87; **Bruce Hogarth** pp.131–133; **Tudor Humphries** p.144; **Iain McIntosh** Introduction, pp.17–19; **Carl Melegari** pp.107, 137, 139; **Ian Miller** pp.83, 86, 106–107, 140–141, 143; **David Parkins** p.9; **Anne Winterbotham** pp.124–126; **Freire Wright** p.76

Cover illustration by Alan Curless
The illustrations on pp.86–87 are produced courtesy of Granada Publishing Ltd.

I should like to offer my grateful thanks to my wife, Brenda, who did the cooking and to my sons John and David whose idea the book was. I should also like to acknowledge my indebtedness to Ron Heapy of the Oxford University Press for his help and encouragement, and to his children, Teresa and Joseph for their interest and enthusiasm; to Rita Winstanley of the University Press for her imaginative design; and to Rosemarie Pitts and Hilary Janes for their work on picture research and illustration.

RJH
Abingdon 1984

Introduction

Goblins and ghosties and long-legged beasties, and things that go bump in the night . . . does your flesh creep and your spine tingle at the very mention of such things?

Well, if you don't go to pieces at the thought of the scarey or creepy, then this is just the book for you. And even if you are of a nervous disposition, then this may still be the book for you because it sets out to explain the origins of spooky occasions like Hallowe'en, the history of witches, and many of the reasons why people think they see ghosts.

I don't know about you but I've never actually seen a ghost even though I've been to places that are famous for them. I once slept in the haunted bedroom of an old inn at Chester, but nothing happened.

I've never had the good luck to see an elf or a fairy or the bad luck to come across a goblin or a demon. As for werewolves and vampires, well, I find it hard to believe that anyone turns into a savage wolf or behaves like a bloodsucking bat.

I did once meet a person who said she was a witch. It was at a pretty dull party and when I asked her if she'd liven things up by turning someone into a toad, she just looked at me coldly and went off to talk to someone else.

Well, at least I didn't ask her where she'd parked her broomstick! Enjoy the creepy book.

party

There is a special time late in the year before the cold raw nights of winter set in, when it is still warm enough to go outside and feel the darkness.

This is the season for you to have a spooky party. People have been holding celebrations at this time of the year for over two thousand years, so you will continuing a very ancient tradition—even if some of the things you do won't have much in common with what happened in days gone by.

In this book there are a number of ideas for you to follow to make your party go really well. There are details about weird invitations, hints on creating a spooky room, tips on dressing up, ideas for ghostly games to play, instructions for making things, and suggestions for preparing ghoulish food.

You will have good fun if you set about getting the party ready well in advance. It will be all the better if you join forces with a friend or two, and ask grown-ups to help with some of the more complicated preparations.

And when you play some of the traditional games and follow a few of the time-honoured activities described in these pages, you will understand a little more how people thought and felt in early times when they feared the darkness much more than we do nowadays....

HALLOWE'EN

All Hallowe'en

Witch and warlock all abroad
Revels keep by field and yard.

In the firelight of the farm
Boy and maiden one by one
Place their chestnuts in the grate
And for omens quietly wait;
To a string their apples tie,
Twirl them till they fallen lie;
Those whose fruits fall in a hurry,
They shall be the first to marry.

Witch and warlock all abroad
Revels keep by field and yard.

Apples from the beam hang down
To be caught by mouth alone,
Mugs of ale on Nut-Crack Night
And many a tale of ghost and sprite,
Come to cheer and chill the heart,
While the candles faint and start,
While the flickering firelight paints
Pictures of the hallowed saints.

Witch and warlock all abroad
Revels keep by field and yard.

Pauline Clark

The origins of Hallowe'en

The word *hallow* means *saint* or *holy person*, and Hallowe'en is short for All Hallows' Eve, the evening before All Hallows' or All Saints' Day, 1 November.

How is it that we celebrate Hallowe'en by thinking of witches, goblins, ghosts and spooks, and don't associate it at all with saints and holy people?

To find the answer we have to go back over 2,000 years. At this point in the year, the ancient Celts held their great autumn festival which marked the end of autumn and the beginning of winter.

For the Celts, this was the end of the old year and the start of the new; and their festival, called Samhain (meaning summer's end), celebrated the time when winter and their new year started together.

The ceremonies at Samhain were conducted by the priests of the Celtic people, men called Druids. This was the time of the year when everything in nature withered and died, and so the Druids performed magic rites and offered sacrifices to their gods to make sure that life and new growth would return in the spring.

The Druids believed that all life came from the underworld and that this was where the spirits of vegetation and growing things went during the winter.

At Samhain the barriers between this world and the underworld were opened. The spirits of the human dead revisited their homes, and gods and strangers from the underworld walked abroad.

The Celts thought that each day ended

at sundown and that a new day began with the coming of darkness. Samhain lasted for two days. It began at dusk on the evening which we know as Hallowe'en, 31 October, and ended on 2 November.

The festival began with the lighting of huge bonfires. These fires were lit to drive away evil spirits, to honour the sun, and to give thanks to the gods that crops and fruits had been gathered in and safely stored for the winter months ahead.

The fires also guided the souls of the dead on their journey back from the underworld. People thought that the ghosts of their dead relatives returned to comfort themselves at the fire before facing the cold and loneliness of the coming winter.

As Christianity grew and spread, many of the pagan customs and festivals continued but they were given new names and meanings to fit in with Christian beliefs. For example, the great midwinter festival of the sun held at the end of December was given over to Christmas. Easter and Holy Week replaced the pagan festivities that celebrated the return of life and growth in the spring.

The Christian leaders, however, were not able to think of a good way to make the autumn festival a part of the Church's calendar, and people went on observing the festival even though the magic rites and ceremonies practised by the Druids were long forgotten.

What was not forgotten was the belief that this was a supernatural time when ghosts and spirits roamed abroad and when dark powers and forces were at work.

At last, in AD 837 the Church leaders decided to dedicate 1 November to the memory of all the saints in heaven and to all those whom the Church had hallowed (or made holy). The day was called All Hallows' Day.

But the belief was still strongly rooted in people's minds that the souls of the human dead revisited their earthly homes at this time. So the Church called 2 November All Souls' day. It was hoped that people would say masses for their loved ones who had died and say prayers for them.

As the centuries went by, people did not grow any less superstitious. They went on thinking of Hallowe'en as a time when witches and demons were active, when elves and fairies came out of their haunts, and when ghosts and spirits made an appearance.

Hallowe'en lanterns

One of the best-known symbols of Hallowe'en is the turnip or pumpkin lantern. In some places these lanterns are known as *Jack o' Lanterns*, in other places they are called *punkies*, or *punky lanterns*.

No one really knows when the tradition of making these lanterns began, but it is believed that their origins go back for thousands of years.

Stone-carved Celtic heads like this one found in Yorkshire, date back for 2,300 years. Heads like this one were placed above doorways to protect the dwelling from harm.

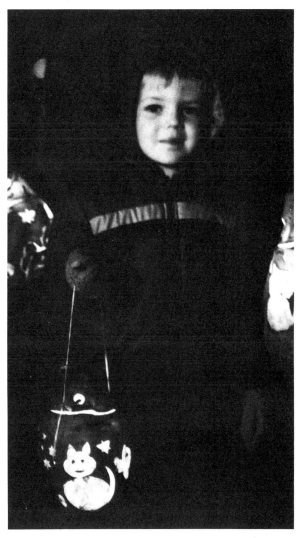

One of the children from the village of Hinton St George, in Somerset, carrying punky lanterns.

It is known that the ancient Celts regarded the human head as a fertility symbol and a charm against evil. The severed heads of enemies, or stone and wooden carvings of human heads were placed in the doorways to protect homes and places of worship.

Lanterns, carved in the form of heads, were probably used by the Celtic Druids at their special Festival of the Dead as a guard against evil spirits and as a welcome to the souls of loved ones who revisited earth at that time.

It is widely believed that in much later times the face-lanterns were meant to frighten away any witches who might ride by at Hallowe'en on their way back from their meeting with the Devil.

As time went by, small groups of people carrying such lanterns would go round the village, especially to scare off witches and evil spirits. However, just to be on the safe side, and as a protection against meeting a particularly nasty spirit who might recognize them later, the lantern-carriers would disguise themselves by blackening their faces or by wearing masks.

The use of a disguise as a protection against evil can be traced back to pagan times when masks and blackened faces were worn by those taking part in rituals to honour the seasons of the year.

In Scotland another name for a Will o' the Wisp is a *spunkie*, while in Somerset a Will o' the Wisp is known as a spunky. It is easy to see why the name punkie, or punky, was given to a turnip lantern.

In some parts of the USA pumpkin lanterns are also called *punkies*. Perhaps this is a combination of the name *spunkie* and *pumpkin*.

In the US, children take great care in selecting pumpkins for Hallowe'en. They hold pumpkin sales and visit pumpkin fields. Once chosen, the pumpkin is carved into a lantern ready for the great night.

Hallowe'en

Witch's fiddle, turnip middle,
Scoop it all out with a spoon.
Curve mouth and eyes
With a careful knife
Beneath the Hallowe'en moon.

Witch-broom handle, long wax candle,
Stick spell-firm in a hole.
Find a match,
Step back and watch,
Hushed as a Hallowe'en mole.

Witch-keen sight, strike bright light,
Match to the greasy wick.
See faint flame
Flick and falter,
Rise and stutter,
Part of the Hallowe'en game.

Witch-black cat; put turnip hat
Gently back on top.
Turn out all moon.
Watch yellow eyes,
Mouth's flamed rays.
Hark for a Hallowe'en tune.

> For the witch's fiddle
> And the witch's cat
> And the crack
> Of a witch-broom handle,
> Sing a haggard song
> On a moonless night
> To a turnip lantern candle.

John Kitching

a hallowe'en lantern

To make a turnip lantern you need a large root such as a swede, a beet, or a mangel. These are the kind of roots which have a reddish skin and yellow flesh.

The skin of these turnips can be carved (or scribed) to make a pattern that will glow when a small candle or flashlight is placed inside the lantern.

You will need:
a small kitchen knife
a metal spoon
a modelling knife
a length of soft wire

1 Carefully cut into the flesh with the kitchen knife to the depth of about 2 cm (¾"), keeping the walls of the lantern about 7 mm (¼") thick. Be careful not to go too deep when cutting your edge: Fig. 1

2 Draw the knife all over the flesh many times, keeping it at a constant depth so that the flesh becomes loosened. You will now be able to scoop out the first 2 cm (¾") with the spoon.

3 Repeat this process taking care not to cut too near the skin. You will find that once a fair-sized cavity has been hollowed out, you will be able to carve out the rest with the spoon.

4 Draw a pattern on the skin with a hard pencil, then carve the skin with the modelling knife, taking care not to cut too deeply. Fig. 2

5 Make a handle with the wire and place a night-light or small flashlight inside the lantern ready for lighting on Hallowe'en.

Fig. 2

Don't try to make the turnip lantern if you are not used to handling a knife. Ask a grown-up to do it for you.

Fig. 1

Why trick or treat?

Mischief Night

Until about a hundred years ago, another name for Hallowe'en, in many parts of Britain, was Mischief Night. Because witches and ghosts were supposed to be abroad on that night, and all kinds of strange and unearthly things were likely to happen, children and young people would use this as an excuse to play tricks and practical jokes on people—especially those they didn't like.

Gates were taken off their hinges, turf would be laid over cottage chimneys so that the fire would smoke, signs and notices were removed, anything found lying about outside was hidden, syrup was smeared on door handles.

In a few places, Mischief Night was held on 4 November. It was particularly popular in Yorkshire and in parts of Scotland, but gradually the practice died out after some of the 'mischief makers' began to take their tricks and practical jokes too far.

In the USA children have observed a more civilized form of Mischief Night, called 'Trick or Treat'. The children dress in Hallowe'en costume and call on neighbours asking them for a treat. Unwilling households have a friendly trick played on them.

All Souls' Day

The day which follows All Saints' Day (1 November) is called All Souls' Day (2 November). This is the day set aside by the Church for people to remember the dead and pray for the souls of ordinary people.

In many villages in Britain it became the custom for poor people to go round collecting gifts of money or food. In return they were expected to say extra prayers for the souls of their rich neighbours' loved ones who had died.

In time the custom became more organized and small groups of people would dress up and parade through the streets singing a soul song. The song asked for gifts, including cakes called *souling cakes* or *soul cakes* which were specially baked for the occasion.

Tonight we come a'souling, good nature to find,
And we hope you'll remember it's a soul-caking time.

In some places the soulers carried the skull of a horse fixed to a pole. This was called the hodening horse and it was supposed to bring good luck to all generous and welcoming households.

Gradually the custom died out although, until quite recent times, children carried on the tradition by calling from door to door, hoping for a cake or a sweet in return for singing a souling song.

It is probably this custom, as much as any other, that has led to the modern-day trick-or-treat practice of giving small gifts to children who call on Hallowe'en.

The hodening horse appears in this version of a soul-caking play performed by the Antrobus mummers at Antrobus in Cheshire.

Trick or Treat

Trick or treat is a game which is most enjoyed by young children. It is fun to call at someone's house if you are dressed up in a Hallowe'en costume. Friends or neighbours are usually happy to join in the fun.

Here are some rules to remember if you go on Trick or Treat:

1 Never, never call at strange houses. Only play Trick or Treat on people with whom you are friendly.

2 Only call if you are dressed up in Hallowe'en costume. Why should people treat you if you can't be bothered to play properly?

3 Don't call on people (especially old people) whom you know don't like opening the door at night.

4 Never play tricks which are messy, frightening, or cause damage. People won't be pleased if they have to spend time, and perhaps money, in clearing up after a silly trick.

5 You are hoping to get something for nothing.

Why should anybody give you anything? So be grateful, and don't forget to say 'thank you'.

Here are some harmless tricks you can play:

1 Tap someone's window by hanging a button over the glass and pulling it on a long thread from a distance.

2 Stick a piece of sticky-tape over someone's bell-push so that the bell goes on ringing.

3 Hang a huge sheet of black plastic over someone's front door (use black plastic bin-liners and fix with sticky tape). Then knock on the door and wait to see what happens.

4 Invent a trick letter that looks all right from one end, but is attached by the other to a great length of card, old paper, or material. Fix it up so that the victim only see the 'good end', then put it in his letter box.

5 Sit on someone's shoulders. Wear a grown-up's hat and a long coat, then call on someone.

6 Tie someone's doormat to some long, black thread. Hide, then when they open the door, pull the mat away.

Requesting the pleasure of

Make some special invitation cards for your spooky party. Here are some ideas for you to copy.

You can make all these cards from strong paper, but if you can afford to buy some sheets of thin card from a stationers of art suppliers, you will get better results.

Use the outlines on pages 18 and 19 of this book. Draw them on to a piece of thick card and cut out; then use as templates to draw round.

To make the coffin

Cut out the coffin shape twice and glue the two pieces together along the coffin side, allowing the lid to lift open. Paint the coffin and write your message under the lid.

To make the skull, cauldron, spook, or bat

Make your template and draw two outlines side by side (or draw the shape once on a folded piece of card) so that the shape is doubled and hinges open.

Paint or colour the outside and write your invitation inside.

To make the pop-out card

For this you will need to use thin card.

Draw a spook or a bat out of card and paint it.

Cut a door big enough to fit the spook or bat in a piece of card, so that the door will open to a fold down one side. **Fig. 1**

Glue this piece of card to another of the same size, taking care not to glue down the door. **Fig. 2**

Cut out a strip of card about 6 cm long by 2 cm wide (2½″ × ¾″). Fold this evenly in concertina fashion.

When you think that the folded card is springy enough, glue the bat or spook to one end and glue the whole thing in the doorway of the card. Make a small flap to keep the door shut. When the door is open, the bat will spring out. **Fig. 3**

You could make the coffin with a pop-out skull using this idea.

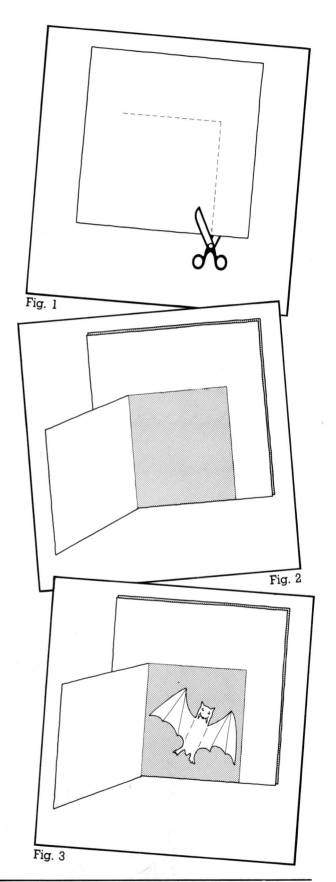

Fig. 1

Fig. 2

Fig. 3

a spooky room

Your party will be all the better if you have it where you can create a weird and spooky atmosphere. You may be lucky enough to have a room which you can decorate with cut-out skeletons, bats, flying witches, spooks, and spiders. At the back of this book you will find a number of shapes which you can enlarge and use as templates to make mobiles and wall decorations.

A word of warning: be sure to have permission before hanging things on walls and ceilings. Sticky-tape, if used, may pull off paintwork and tear wallpaper, so ask a grown-up for advice.

Ways to transform the walls

Cut open large black plastic bin-liners and join the sections into strips using sticky-tape. Hang these strips round the walls, so that the room is lined with black. Fix black paper (or bin-liner) to the door; alternatively use grey or brown paper and paint on it to transform the door into the entrance to a tomb, vault, or chamber.

You'll find that the black walls make an effective background against which to hang white shapes, such as skeletons and spooks. You can also paint on the black plastic with white emulsion paint.

Paste together three or four large sheets of newspaper (use fairly thick wallpaper paste) and allow them to dry slowly. Then paint skulls or weird faces on them, using powder or poster paint, or emulsion paints. Cut the shapes out and hang them on the walls. By joining a number of sheets of paper you can make an area large enough to paint a spooky mural.

Light the room with dim coloured lighting. You can do this by painting low wattage bulbs with thick poster paints.

The dancing skeleton

A skeleton like the one on this page will look good hanging on your black wall, or against any black background. You can use white construction card, but it is cheaper to use unwanted boxes from a foodstore.

At the back of the book you will find the outline of a skeleton to copy. It is drawn on a grid. You can increase the size of your figure by drawing a much larger grid on card and copying the shapes in exactly the same position on the squares. Fig. 1.

Fasten the skeleton together at those points that are marked on the outline with an X using paper fasteners. Fig. 2. Paint the skeleton with white and black poster or emulsion paints.

You can make the skeleton dance by hanging it up on a piece of cord elastic. Fix a weight behind the ribs (a spanner held on by sticky tape will do). Tie lengths of thread between the fixing point on the wall and the skeleton's arms and legs. This will make the limbs dance as the skeleton bounces up and down. Fig. 3. If you attach a long piece of thread to the body and trail it to another part of the room, you can make the skeleton appear to dance all by itself when you pull secretly on the thread.

Spooky sentiments

Make up sinister slogans, nasty notices or ghastly graffiti to go round your spooky room. You can write these on paper placards or paint them directly on to your black plastic bin liners.

The best-known spooky sentence is 'Abandon Hope All Ye Who Enter Here' and this may be put up to good effect over the doorway of your room.

You may like to put up comic slogans such as 'Fangs for the Memory', or 'Welcome Boys and Ghouls'. You may like something a little more spine-chilling such as 'The Chamber of Horror' or 'Fear Rules Tonight.'

a dancing skeleton

Fig. 1

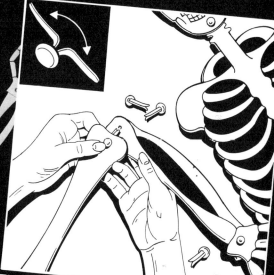

Fig. 2

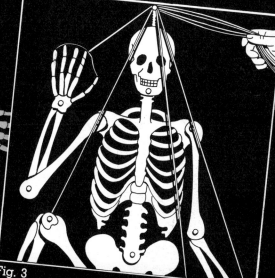

Fig. 3

a spider's web

Cut black plastic bin liners into narrow, jagged strips about 50 cm (20″) long. Hang the strips lengthwise from the ceiling. Alternatively, hang strips cut from old nylon stockings or tights, or from clear plastic, or aluminium foil.

Use the shape on page 19 and make a brood of bats to hang from the ceiling.

If you have a picture-rail, or somewhere to tie string, you can make a huge cobweb. Start with the central ring, making a loop of string about 50 cm (20″) in diameter. Fig. 1.

Fig. 1.

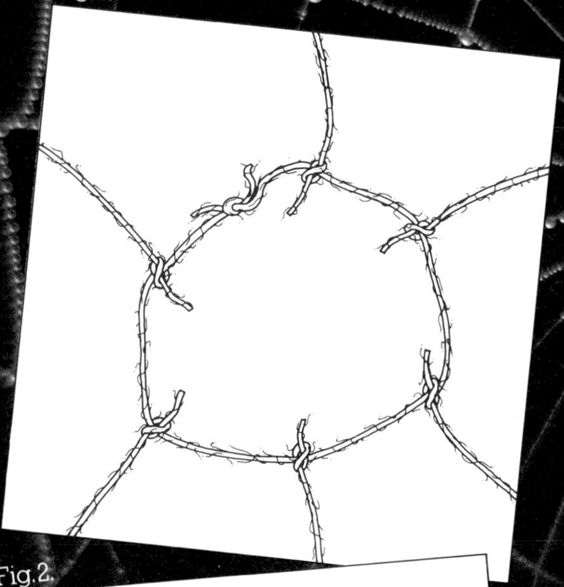

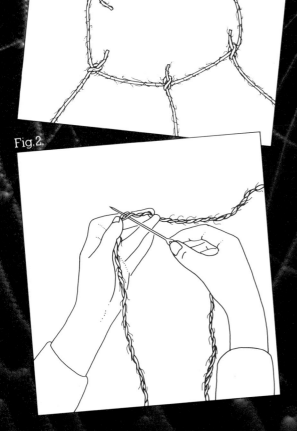

Fig. 2.

To the loop tie eight to ten lengths of string long enough to reach your fixing points on the walls. Tie the string loosely at first, then adjust and tighten until the central ring is a good shape.

You'll need six or eight rings to make your cobweb look effective. Use a fairly thick jute string, and you'll be able to untwist the strands to thread the string through. This is best done using a needle with a very large eye. Fig. 2.

Do not make the rings look too even. Colour the points where the strings cross with thick poster or powder paints.

Fix spiders and bats to the cobweb and hang black thread from it, sufficiently long to brush against your guests' faces.

HOW TO MAKE
a mask

If you dress up for your party you may decide that the easiest thing will be to buy a mask from a novelty store in order to give your face the appearance you require.

You'll probably find a good selection of masks to choose from, such as a witch, devil, phantom, ghoul, zombie, skull, monster, Count Dracula, the Frankenstein Monster and so on.

You may, however, want to make your appearance completely unique by devising your own mask. You will get a great deal of enjoyment and satisfaction from creating something all of your own, but if you decide to do this, prepare it in plenty of time otherwise you may be disappointed. You'll probably have to experiment as you may not get the results you hoped for the first time.

You will need

a large round balloon
newspaper
wallpaper paste
scissors
2.5 cm (1″) paintbrush
paints and felt tips

Begin by tearing the newspaper into small pieces about 4 cm (2″) square. Blow up your balloon and make up a thick wallpaper paste in a jam jar (use about a tablespoon of powder).

Paste the pieces of paper to the balloon so that the edges just overlap (fig. 1). Be systematic about this or you'll get a difference in thickness. You'll need about three or four layers of newspaper. If you get folds or crease-crinkles, snip them carefully with fine scissors and paste them flat.

Allow the covered balloon to dry slowly. Don't put it near any source of heat to dry.

Deflate and remove the balloon, then cut the shape you require (fig. 2). You can 'tailor' the mask by cutting, overlapping the cut edges, and then re-sticking.

To fit a nose, use a single section from an egg-box cut lengthways. Paste this over a hole cut in the mask, using newspaper layers (fig. 3).

When the mask is dry, paint it. To achieve a flesh colour, add white powder or poster paint to burnt sienna until you get the tone you need. (Don't use red or pink paint for flesh colouring.)

Ask a grown-up to let you finish off with a coat of clear varnish.

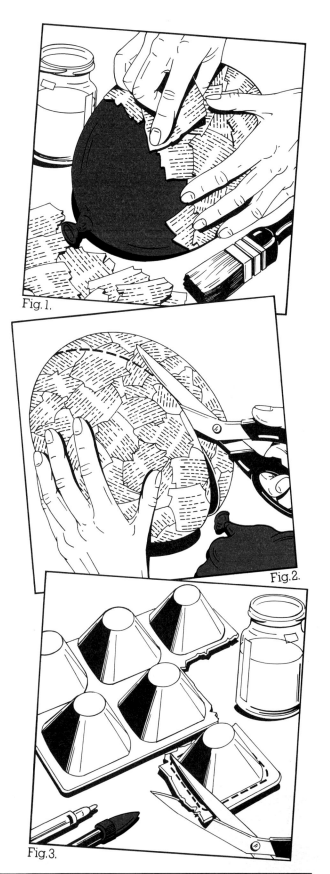

Fig. 1.

Fig. 2.

Fig. 3.

HOW TO MAKE
a skull costume

You will need:

    a white nylon stocking
    a white bathing cap (boys' type)
    a ping-pong ball
    black felt-tips
    black and white powder paint (or stage make-
       up)
    small round plastic tub
    talcum powder.

To make the eye sockets

Use two halves of the ping-pong ball. Shape each half to fit comfortably over the eyes.
Cut out two small eye-holes. Paint or colour them black .

To make the jaw

Cut segments from the bottom of a small white plastic tub. (You can grip the plastic with your teeth, but this can become uncomfortable, so make a flap that will fit under your lips.) Draw teeth on to one face of each segment ready to fit both into your mouth.

To create the face

Put on the white bathing cap. (If you can't get one, dust your hair with talcum powder.) Whiten your face with stage make-up, white powder paint, or powder. Darken the nose with black paint, and make grey shadows round the eyes and down the cheeks.

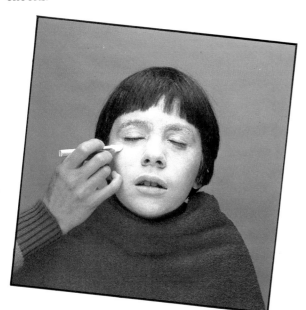

Place the eye sockets on your eyes and grip the plastic jaw with your lips.

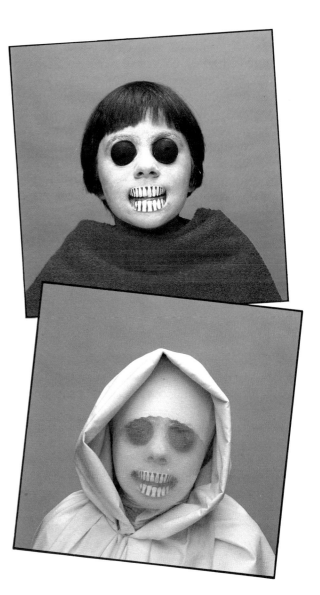

Pull the nylon stocking over your head. Neaten it up, and touch up your face with make-up or paint where necessary.

HOW TO MAKE

a ghoul costume

You will need:
- a flesh-coloured stocking
- two ping-pong balls
- cotton-wool or lint
- nylon and felt tips
- poster or powder paints
  (red, black, white, burnt sienna)
- needle and thread.

To make the eye-socket

From the cotton wool or lint, cut out a flat oval pad about 4 cm × 5 cm (1¾″ × 2″). Shape it like an eye-patch to fit completely round your eye.

Mix white and burnt sienna to make a flesh colour and paint the outside of the pad. When this is dry, paint the centre of the pad black and, round that, paint an uneven red edge. Fig. 1.

To make the eyes

For the good eye, use half a ping-pong ball.
Use a whole ping pong ball for the eyeball. Draw in the pupil and iris in black and blue or green. Draw in a network of fine red veins. Attach a white cotton thread to the back of the eyeball. Fig. 2.

To create the face

Draw scars and stitches, using felt tips, onto the nylon stocking.
Place the ping-pong ball eye in one eye, and the eye-socket pad over the other. Put some trickles of red paint from the eye socket down the cheek.
Pull the stocking over the head, making sure that your hair is pushed out of the way.
Touch up your face with paint where necessary. Attach the eyeball from the centre of the eye socket by the white thread. Fig. 3.

The slimy monster

To make yourself into a slimy monster attach pieces of shiny green plastic torn from a plastic bag to a green or white nylon stocking mask. Allow the torn pieces to hang in jagged, uneven fronds.

Stick pieces of green coloured dough (or nose paste) unevenly to your cheeks using copydex or latex glue. The dough can be coloured with green food-colouring.

Make ping-pong ball eyes, and a weirdly-shaped plastic tub mouth.

Pull the stocking over your face and touch up with paint or make-up where necessary.

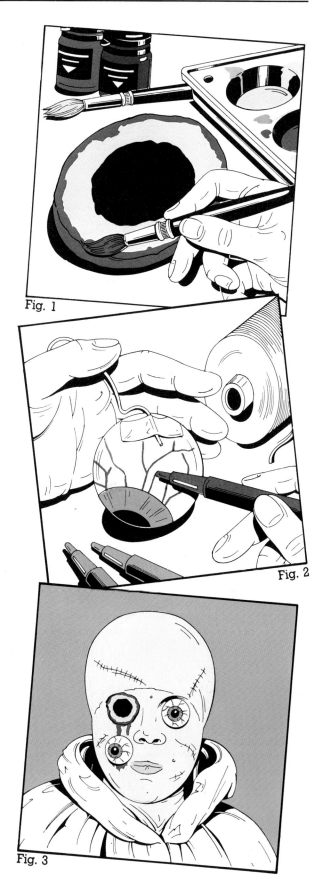

Fig. 1

Fig. 2

Fig. 3

Apples

The magical fruit

In ancient times the apple was thought of as a holy or magical fruit. The idea in the old saying, 'An apple a day keeps the doctor away', may have come from the Norse legend which tells how the gods kept their health and youth by eating the apples which grew in the garden of Asgard, their home in the sky. The Celts believed in a paradise where apple trees carried fragrant blossom and ripe fruit at one and the same time. According to the old beliefs of the Iroquois Indians, the apple was the central tree of heaven. We think of the forbidden fruit eaten by Eve in the Garden of Eden as the apple, although in the Authorized Version of the Bible it is simply called 'the fruit of the tree'.

Your fortune in love

Apples played an important part in games played at Hallowtide where young people tried to find out their fortune in love. One game was for each person to tie an apple on

26

a piece of string and spin it round and round. The one whose apple flew off first would be the first to marry. Anyone whose apple failed to come off would die unwed. If an apple was peeled in one long unbroken strip and the peel thrown over the left shoulder, the shape it took on the ground would show the initial letter of a girl's future husband. Some girls would cut an apple into nine slices and stick the slices on to the blade of a knife. Then they would hold the slices over their left shoulder, while combing their hair in front of a mirror. A vision of a girl's future husband was then supposed to appear in the mirror.

Wassailing parties

In apple-growing districts, such as Devon and Somerset, it is still the custom to hold special ceremonies each winter to encourage the growth of apples in the coming year. These ceremonies are called 'Wassailing Parties'. The wassailers go into the orchards and drink the health of every tree. Then everyone throws part of the drink, followed by stones or even gunshot, through the bare branches of the trees. It was once thought that this would drive out any evil spirits in the orchard.

Superstitions

There are many strange old customs and superstitions to do with apples. It was thought that if the sun shone through the branches of the apple trees on Christmas morning, the trees would produce plenty of fruit in the year to come. In many places it was considered unlucky, when the fruit was being picked, to strip every apple off the tree. An apple or two should be left behind as a gift for the birds. In other places people believed that if an apple left on the tree was still there when spring came round there would be a death in the family.

apple games

Games using apples have always been played at Hallowe'en. Try some of these at your party.

Bob Apple (or Apple Ducking)

This is a very well-known game. All you need is a large tub of water (a clean plastic washing-up bowl will do), and a large plastic sheet to cover the floor.

Float a few apples in the water. The players kneel in front of the bowl with their hands tied behind their backs and try to pick up an apple with their teeth.

Snap Apple

Apples are suspended from the ceiling on a long piece of string (in a doorway would do). Players have to eat the apple, which must not be touched by any other part of the body, except the teeth. (In some places the apples in this game are smeared with golden syrup or jam to make the thing messy but more fun!)

Tilt Apple

For this game, players pick an apple out of the water and eat it using the handles of two forks, or better still, using two fairly thin sticks about 30 cm (12″) long.

Pips

Apple pips were also used as love signs. When a girl had two men to choose from she would get two pips, call each one after the two lovers, then stick the pips on her cheek. The pip which fell off first was the man she should reject. Another game was to put an apple pip on the bars of a fire. If the pip burst in the heat with a loud pop it meant that the girl's lover would be true, but if the pip just burned slowly it meant he would not be faithful.

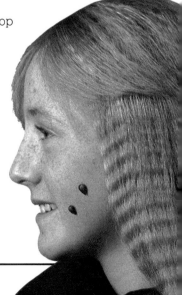

German Apple cake

This German recipe will give a delicious cake which can be served warm or cold.

You will need:

  1 lb (450 g) apples
  2–3 eggs
  4 oz (125 g) sugar
  4 oz (125 g) butter
  1–4 tablespoons of milk
  7 oz (200 g) self-raising flour
  4 drops lemon flavouring.

Wooden spoon, mixing bowl, 8″ (20 cm) cake tin.

Mix the butter, sugar and eggs. Add lemon flavouring.

Mix in the flour with the milk until the mixture is of a soft dropping consistency.

Put the mixture into the greased tin.

Peel and cut apples into quarters. Score with a knife to decorate, and place the scored surface uppermost on top of the mixture.

Bake for about 45 minutes (Gas mark 4 Reg 375°F)

Dust before serving with icing sugar (confectioners' sugar).

Chocolate Apple Sauce Cake

This delicious American recipe gives a lovely moist cake which you can serve at your party.

You will need:
1 cup (6oz) of margarine
1 cup (6oz) of sugar
1 egg
1 cup of unsweetened apple compote made from 4 large cooking apples
1½ cups (8oz) + 2 tablespoons of plain flour
½ cup (2oz) of cocoa
1½ teaspoons of cinnamon
1 teaspoon bicarbonate of soda
1 teaspoon of water
a bar of plain chocolate.

Wooden spoon, mixing bowl, sieve, greased baking tin.

Cream the margarine with the sugar.

Add beaten egg.

Put in the apple compote.

Sieve flour, cocoa, cinnamon together and add to the mixture. Stir the mixture well.

Dissolve the bicarbonate of soda in the water, add to the mixture and stir thoroughly.

Bake in a greased tin (Gas mark 4 Reg 375°F) for about ½ an hour or until soft to the touch.

When cool, spread melted chocolate on the top. Cut into slices when the chocolate has set.

Toffee apples

You will need:
4–6 small soft eating apples
8 oz (225 g) loaf sugar
½ lemon
4 tablespoons water
knob of butter.
wooden skewers or peeled sticks
a platter or baking tray
saucepan
wooden spoon.

Wash and dry the apples. Fix them on the skewers or sticks.

Butter the platter or baking tray.

Put the sugar, a squeeze of lemon and 4 tablespoons of water into the pan and place on a low heat, stirring until dissolved.

Now boil fast until golden brown.
Don't take your eyes off the mixture for a second while doing this.

When you judge the mixture to be brown enough, take the pan from the heat. Work quickly. Turn the apples into the sugar mixture, turning to make sure each is completely covered. Be careful not to get any of the hot toffee on your fingers.

Leave the toffee apples to harden on the buttered platter.

Toffee apples are a nice idea to serve at any party. If you decide to make your own **be very careful**. The hot toffee can leave a nasty burn if you drop any on your skin. Make sure a grown-up helps you.

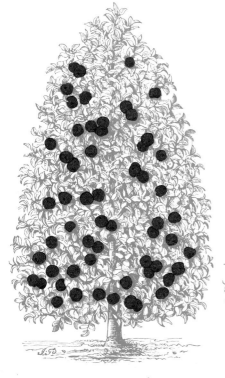
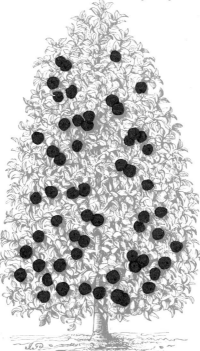
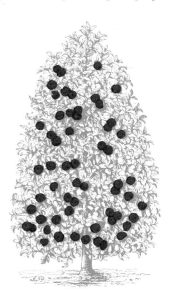

How to make pumpkin pie

(or what to do with the inside of your pumpkin lantern)

You will need:

- 8 oz (225 g) shortcrust pastry
- 1 tablespoonful sesame seeds
- 2 eggs slightly beaten
- 2 cups of cooked and drained pumpkin
- 1 cup of evaporated milk
- ¼ cup of golden syrup
- 2 oz (50 g) butter
- ½ cup of brown sugar
- ¼ teaspoonful salt
- 1½ teaspoonsful cinnamon
- ¼ teaspoonful nutmeg
- ⅛ teaspoonful ground cloves.

Add the sesame seeds to the pastry when making it, and line a 8″ (20 cm) pie dish.

Combine the pumpkin, syrup, egg, and half of the evaporated milk.

Heat the rest of the milk with the butter, then add to the pumpkin mix with the sugar and spices.

Pour into the pastry case and bake (Gas mark 8 Reg 450°F) for 15 minutes. Reduce to Gas mark 4 (Reg 375°F) for 40 minutes, or until set.

Serve cold with whipped cream.

Bonfire Pie

This savoury supper dish would be ideal to serve after a bonfire party or at Hallowe'en if there are only a few people. The quantity in this recipe serves four.

You will need:

- 1 lb (450g) chipolata sausages (pork)
- 8 oz (225g) stewed apple
- 3 large onions
- 8 oz (225g) tomatoes—or small can
- small can peas
- 2 oz (50 g) grated cheese
- 2 lb (900g) approx mashed potatoes

Grease an ovenproof dish (a large flat one if possible).

Place in layers onions, skinned sausages, stewed apple, sliced tomatoes, and peas.

Spread or pipe potatoes over them, and add grated cheese.

Cook in a hot oven (Gas mark 8 Reg 450°F) for about three-quarters of an hour.

31

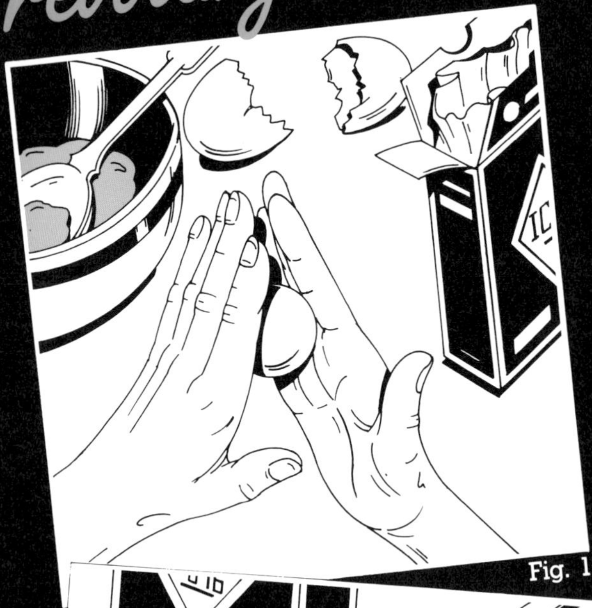

revolting sweets

Fig. 1

Fig. 2

Spooky Eyeballs

You will need:

> 1 lb (500 g) icing sugar (confectioner's sugar)
> 1 egg-white
> peppermint essence
> a black liquorice sweet
> blue or green colouring
> Egg-cup, saucer, wooden spoon, mixing bowl,
> greaseproof paper, metal spoon, sieve.

Beat the egg-white lightly, and blend with sifted icing sugar and a few drops of peppermint essence. Mix in icing sugar until you get a fine dry paste.

Using finger-tips, knead the paste, adding small amounts of icing sugar for as long as the paste will absorb it.

Separate a small quantity to make the irises of your spooky eyeballs. Add a few drops of blue or green colouring and mix in with a metal spoon.

Roll the white mixture into small round balls. (You can do this easily if you sprinkle a little icing sugar on to the palms of your hands.) Fig. 1. Press a hole in the top of the ball with your little finger or the end of the wooden spoon.

Make a flat button-shape with the coloured mixture big enough to fit in to the hole.

Cut out a small round section of the liquorice sweet to make the pupil. Fig. 2.

Mice and Frogs

Use the egg-white and icing-sugar mix to make these sugar mice and frogs.

You will need:

egg-white and icing-sugar mix, flavoured with peppermint essence if preferred.
a few drops of green or blue colouring (to colour the mice and frogs).
tiny sweets, such as jelly-tots for the frogs' eyes
string to make the tails and whiskers of the mice.

Mould the body of a mouse in a large teaspoon or small dessertspoon. Make a head for the mouse and fix on to the body. Use a small length of string for the tail and short strands of string for the whiskers. Place a tiny piece of sweet for the eye. Fig. 1.

Shape the frog's body as shown. Use yellow or green jelly-tot sweets for the eyes. Fig. 2.

Fig. 1

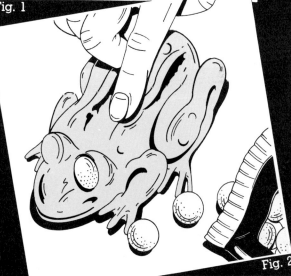

Fig. 2

Fire and Brimstone

Use a little of the egg-white and icing-sugar mix to make some of these revolting sweets.

You will need:

a small quantity of egg-white and icing-sugar mix
a small quantity of curry powder
(for the brimstone)
a tiny dash of chilli sauce or a few drops of Worcester sauce
(for the fire)
permission from your parents.

Only add about ⅛ of a teaspoon of curry powder to the sweet mixture. Taste a little when blended in. Do the same with the Worcester sauce. BEWARE! If you use chilli sauce IT IS VERY HOT. Make only small sweets and try to make them look as revolting as possible. Place a 'warning' notice on the plate when serving them.

33

Many of the games played at Hallowe'en in the past were games which were supposed to predict the fortunes of the players during the twelve months of the year that lay ahead.

Three Luggies

Three Luggies is the name of a popular game which was once played in Scotland at Hallowe'en. Three small bowls or luggies were placed on the floor. In one was clear water, in another was muddy water, and the third was empty.

Each boy or young man was blindfolded in turn and told to place his left hand in one of the bowls. The order of the bowls were then changed without him seeing. If he chose the clear water then it meant he would marry a maiden. If he chose muddy water, it meant he would marry a widow, and if he chose the empty bowl then he would never marry at all.

One Mirror

It was once a superstition among young people on Hallowe'en for them to look into a mirror on the stroke of midnight. Instead of seeing their own reflection they would see an image of the person they were supposed to marry. Older people were too scared to look into the mirror in case they saw something frightening.

Twelve Candles

Another Hallowe'en game from Scotland was called Twelve Candles. Candles representing the twelve months of the year were placed on the floor in a wide circle. A player began with January and jumped over every candle in turn.

For each candle still alight at the end of his go, a player could expect a lucky month in the year ahead.

If you play this game, don't use candles. Balance two playing cards on a pile of tins and jump over that.

Young girls try to discover the course of their love affairs by roasting chestnuts. Two nuts are placed side by side on the bars of the fire. If a nut cracks and jumps away it shows that one of the lovers will not be true, but if both nuts blaze away together it is a sign that the lovers will marry. Because of this game Hallowe'en was once known as Nutcrack Night in some parts of Britain.

Morrow's amazing metascope

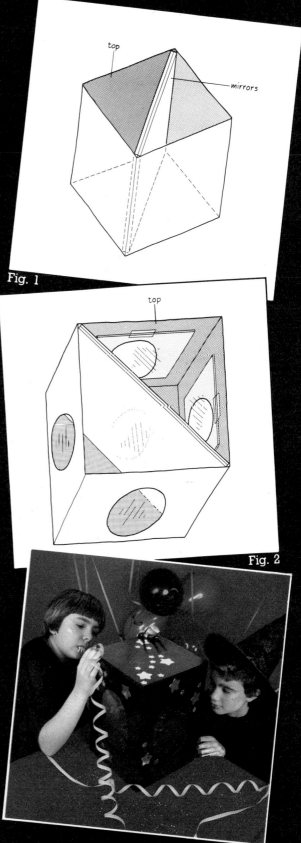

It was once a superstition among young people on Hallowe'en for them to look into a mirror on the stroke of midnight. Instead of seeing their own reflection they would see an image of the person they were supposed to marry. Older people were too scared to look into a mirror in case they saw something frightening.

You can use some 'mirror magic' to amaze your friends at your spooky party. Morrow's Metascope looks, at first glance, like an empty box with four small oval windows.

When four people sit round a table and look into the little windows they are in for a surprise. Each person, instead of seeing his own reflection will see that of the person on his right who, at the same time, will appear to be on the opposite side.

You will need:
two mirror tiles 30.5 cm (12") square
stiff card
black paper (or matt black paint)
glue, scissors, sticky tape
glass or clear pvc.
gold decoration (such as stars or doilies)

You need to make a box approx 22.5 cm (9") square by 30.5 (12") deep in which you will fix two $30.5 \times 30.5 \text{ cm}^2$ ($12'' \times 12''^2$) mirrors diagonally, placing them back to back and standing them upright (fig 1). You may need to adjust the size of your box to accommodate the thickness of the mirrors.

Before fixing the mirrors inside, line the box with black paper or paint with matt black paint.

In each side of the box cut an oval window $18 \times 13.5 \text{ cm}$ ($7'' \times 5\frac{1}{2}''$).

Put a piece of glass over each opening and hold it in place with sticky tape. Fig. 2

Place the mirrors in position and fix on the lid.

Paint the box black and decorate it with gold stars. You may like to make frames for the oval windows with the edges of the gold doilies.

To use the metascope to its best effect, put it at head height, perhaps on a small table, round which four people will be seated. Keep it covered with a cloth and use some 'magician's talk' before you pull the cloth off to reveal the box.

Fig. 1

Fig. 2

chamber of Morbius

Staging a stunt at your spooky party could be fun, providing you have guests with steely nerves, who don't mind being hoaxed. During a stunt the victims wait outside the room, and come in one at a time. After each turn the victims can enjoy watching the stunt being played on the next person to come in.

A good stunt will take quite a lot of preparation. It may involve sound effects, lighting, costume, and special properties, so you will need to work out how much time you want to spend both in setting it up and staging it.

The success of a good stunt depends on the fun and laughter it creates for everyone. Never take advantage of your guests' good nature by making it so frightening or unpleasant that they don't enjoy it.

Here is an example of the kind of stunt you could set up. With imagination and planning you could adapt some of these ideas and add a few more of your own.

The Chamber of Morbius

The victims are sent to wait outside the room. They are told that they will shortly be able to enter the Chamber of Morbius where they will undergo a trial of their courage and fortitude. If they survive the horrors which guard the Chamber they will be allowed to enter the inner sanctum and discover for themselves the secret of Morbius.

Meanwhile, the room is being made ready with whatever props and effects are needed for the stunt.

Then, one by one, the victims knock on the door, which is opened by the doorkeeper. The following dialogue takes place (the victim's answers can be written on a card).

'What seek you?'

'The secret of Morbius.'

'Do you promise to do as you are commanded?'

'I do.'

'Do you promise to ask no questions and to tell no one what you discover?'

'I do.'

'Enter.'

The victim is led into a room which is divided off by screens. (Old sheets could be used for this.) The room is lit by a dim coloured light. Some weird music is playing.

The victim is asked to stand on a short plank which rests on bricks or small boxes. A blindfold is placed over his eyes. His hands are placed on the shoulders of two attendants who stand on either side of him.

He is told that if he is a worthy candidate, the power of Morbius will raise him up into the air. In fact he is such a suitable candidate that his head bumps gently against the ceiling. (The illustration shows you how to do this.)

Safely back on the ground, the victim is asked if

The victim thinks he is rising when the attendants sink slowly down towards the floor while others gently rock the plank. The ceiling is a book which is gently bumped on the victim's head.

he is willing to undergo a test of courage. He is told that he must walk barefoot through the snake pit which guards the entrance to the inner sanctum. No harm will come to him if he has led an honest and completely blameless life.

In the pit is a mass of snakes' eggs. Unfortunately the victim walks over several, which crush beneath his tread. In fact the eggs are simply polystyrene egg-boxes or apple dividers.

The victim is now able to enter the inner sanctum where he is to be asked to hold the brain of Morbius which will allow him to look into the past and future at the same time.

A gong is struck (an old tin tray will do) and the brain is placed in the victim's hands. At the same time the blindfold is removed.

The brain is made from cold, congealed spaghetti.

The impact is considerable, but it soon dissolves into the general laughter which follows. The victim can then join the 'silent' onlookers and enjoy the next candidate for the Chamber of Morbius.

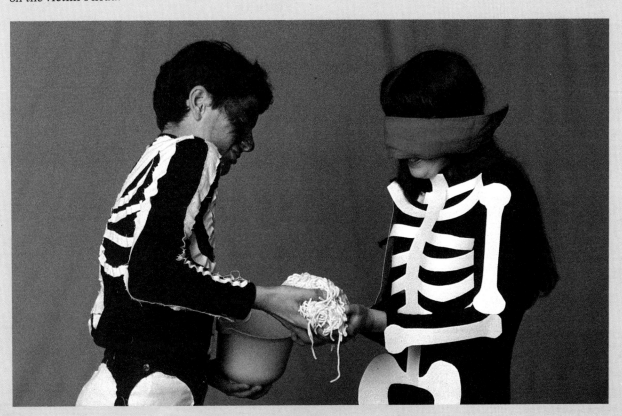

modern party games

The Devil's dollar

Show your guests a coin, which you tell them is the Devil's dollar. Send the guests outside the door for a few seconds while you place the coin somewhere in the room, but not hidden from sight.

The idea of the game is that once a player has spotted the coin, he or she should sit down on the floor (without, of course, making it obvious where the coin is). The last person standing up in each round is out.

The winner of the game is the first person to spot the coin when there are only two players left in. (It is a good idea to let the person who is out each time place the coin to begin each new round of the game.)

Hallowe'en trail

Write on a number of cards, big enough to read fairly easily, the following places:

Count Dracula's castle	A
The chamber of horrors	E
Frankenstein's laboratory	L
The haunted house	C
The graveyard	H
The witch's kitchen	K
The Devil's den	B
Werewolf woods	F
The snake pit	J
The black swamp	D
The vampires' lair	G

Place the cards in various parts of the house (check which rooms you are allowed to use). Send all the players off to find Count Dracula's Castle and return with the letter next to it on the card. As each player comes back with the answer, send him or her off to the next place. The winner is the one to complete the trail first.

Don't squash the eyeball

Play this guessing game by blindfolding either one or all of your guests and giving them some of these gruesome objects to hold.

Here are some ideas for grizzly things to pass round, or to let someone feel as a forfeit:

some stewed apple or mashed potato wrapped in cling-film
a skinned tomato (skin it by dropping it in very hot water)
a handful of cold, cooked spaghetti
a used tea-bag
a balloon or rubber glove partly filled with water
some cooked marrow, pumpkin or squash
a box containing a fur glove (with someone's hand in it!)
an egg cup filled with solid custard.

Only play this game if you know that the carpets, chairs, or people's clothes are protected from being messed up.

Forfeits

Here are some forfeits you can give to your party guests if you play any forfeit games:
suck a slice of lemon
drink a glass of water backwards, i.e. with your mouth on the opposite side of the glass
balance a plastic cup of water on your head and sit on the floor
eat some jelly with your hands tied behind your back
pick up a sweet out of a saucer of flour with your teeth
have an ice-cube or cold spoon down your back.

For younger children:
grunt like a pig
imitate a fish breathing
walk like a chicken
count from 10 to 1 backwards
spin round ten times, then walk in a straight line.

HOW TO MAKE
a tin—can lantern

This tin-can lantern is simple to make, but get a grown-up to help you. You need strong hands to cut out the panels but **be careful:** sharp tin can cut you.

You will need:

 a 15 oz (425 g) tin-can (a soft-drink can will be easier to cut, but it will be less rigid)
 tin snips (or very old strong scissors)
 a jam jar to fit inside the can
 strong wire
 felt-tip pen
 small hammer
 and fine file
 night-light or
 small flashlight
 poster paints.

Wash out and remove the label. Then mark four panels using the felt-tip pen. Fig. 1.

Fig. 1

Place a large piece of wood inside the tin to give support and pierce the side as shown. Fig. 2.

Fig. 2

Cut out the first panel. Fig. 3. If large panels as shown prove difficult to cut, neatly cut out two or three large diamond panels.

Tap down and smooth off any sharp edges and sharp slivers of tin with the hammer and file.

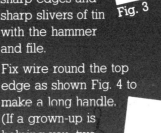

Fig. 3

Fix wire round the top edge as shown Fig. 4 to make a long handle. (If a grown-up is helping you, two holes could be punched in the tin to take the wire, or, better still, it could be soldered on.)

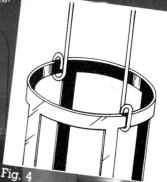

Fig. 4

The great Hallow fires

The coming of winter

For thousands of years people in almost every country of northern Europe have celebrated the beginning of winter by lighting huge bonfires. To the people in ancient times each bonfire was the symbol of light and warmth at a time when the power of the sun was on the wane. Ahead lay the dark months of winter when it seemed that the spirit of growing things departed and the earth became cold and barren.

In Celtic times sacred fires were kindled as part of the ceremony of Samhain (summer's end). These huge fires, lit to mark the end of the Celtic year, also guided the souls of dead loved ones who were able to revisit their homes on this one night. This happened because the gates of the underworld opened to receive the spirits of growing things which departed during winter. However, this allowed evil spirits to roam freely, and so the great fires kept the dark forces at bay.

Ancient customs.

These ancient beliefs were held until quite recent times. In Wales, for example, older people can still remember being told by their grandparents that on All Hallows' Eve the spirit of a departed person could be seen at every crossroad and on every stile. In parts of the north of England a farmer would sometimes light a small fire in his fields, and when it was burning well he would carry some of the burning wood to the four corners of his land. This was to guard against evil and to ensure healthy crops and livestock in the months ahead. Meanwhile his family would kneel round the bonfire and offer prayers for the souls of the dead of their kin. Even today there are fields in the north which are called Purgatory fields because this ancient custom once took place in them.

A guard against evil

Traditionally, Hallowe'en bonfires were lit to drive away witches and warlocks and to prevent visits from devils, demons, and any other kind of evil or unpleasant spirits. Fairies, too, were thought to be roaming freely, and anyone foolish enough to be travelling after nightfall was in danger of being carried off to fairy land to be made to dance without stopping until the next Hallowe'en. In Ireland it was believed that the Cave of Couachar in Connaught, known as the hell-gate of Ireland, was opened and a horde of terrifying fiends and goblins would rush forth, including a flock of ghastly copper-red birds whose breath killed cattle and poisoned the land. In Scotland horrid bogies went about stealing babies and doing all kinds of other nasty things. No wonder people needed the comfort of huge bonfires

Neid fires

In the Highlands of Scotland, the custom of lighting the great Hallow fires was particularly strongly observed. Fire played a very important part in people's lives where there was little or no wood. The fires, called *neid fires*, were lit on cairns. Everyone was expected to give something to build the fire with, since it was lit as a protection against witches. Boys would call at each cottage calling 'Gie's a peat for the witches'. When the fire was blazing, young men would make a sport of jumping over it. As the fire died, they would run through the glowing ashes. On the following day people scattered some of the ashes on their land to bless and purify the land and bring good luck.

The year ahead

In some places it was a tradition, when the fire was at its hottest, for people to throw large stones into the flames. It was important for each person to be able to identify his stone, because the next day the stones would be raked out of the ashes. If a stone had split or fractured it meant an unlucky year for that person in the year that lay ahead.

Guy Fawkes Night

Almost four hundred years ago, an event took place in British history which changed the nature of the great winter bonfires. It caused the decline of the Hallowe'en celebrations in most parts of Britain in favour of a completely different kind of Fire Festival.

The date was 5 November 1605: the discovery, in the nick of time, of the Gunpowder Plot saved King James I and his Parliament from a violent and horrifying death.

In gratitude for its safe delivery, Parliament ordered that this day should be observed as a holiday and general day of rejoicing. The people responded enthusiastically by lighting enormous bonfires on which they burned the effigy of one of the conspirators in the Gunpowder Plot, a man called Guy Fawkes.

From then on the great fires that had previously blazed on Hallowe'en burned instead on 5 November and although the public holiday was ended during the reign of Queen Victoria, Guy Fawkes Night is still as popular as ever.

A Guy Fawkes Celebration at Lewes in Sussex.

In many parts of Britain bonfire parties and firework displays are, to this day, held on or around Guy Fawkes Night (5 November). Friends or neighbours get together in back yards or on waste ground to organize Guy Fawkes Parties.

In some English towns, bonfire celebrations are taken very seriously. At Lewes, in Sussex, the Cliffe Society organize a torchlight procession through the town and on to a high area called the Cliffe where a spectacular bonfire and firework display is held.

HOW TO HAVE

a hallowe'en bonfire

There is something wonderful and exciting about standing round a blazing bonfire on a dark winter's evening. Watching the sparks fly upwards like orange fireflies, smelling the sharp smell of wood-smoke, and listening to the crackle and hiss of burning wood has an irresistible fascination for everyone.

Even if your back-yard is small you can still have a bonfire, providing it is not too large. Your party guests will enjoy standing round even a small fire outside but, of course, you must **not** have a bonfire unless a grown-up is in charge of it.

A word to grown-ups

1 Never let children light a bonfire, or play round one unless you are there to supervise them. A bonfire could be a danger to anyone wearing a cloak or robe as part of a Hallowe'en costume.

2 Never use petrol or gasoline to light a bonfire. Never pour from a can or bottle any volatile fluid on to an ailing bonfire.

3 Treat all fireworks with the greatest caution. Read instructions. Follow the safety code and keep children well clear.

Roast chestnuts or potatoes wrapped in tinfoil in the embers; toast sausages or marshmallows on a stick. If you are unable to light a fire in your yard, then why not have a winter barbecue using charcoal?

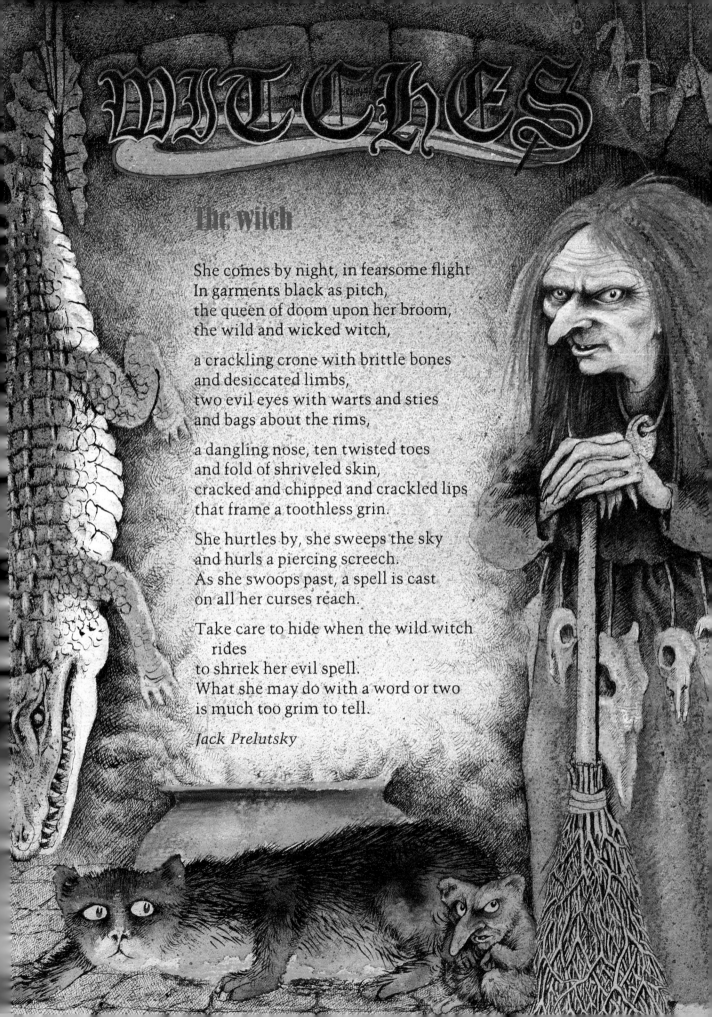

WITCHES

The witch

She comes by night, in fearsome flight
In garments black as pitch,
the queen of doom upon her broom,
the wild and wicked witch,

a crackling crone with brittle bones
and desiccated limbs,
two evil eyes with warts and sties
and bags about the rims,

a dangling nose, ten twisted toes
and fold of shriveled skin,
cracked and chipped and crackled lips
that frame a toothless grin.

She hurtles by, she sweeps the sky
and hurls a piercing screech.
As she swoops past, a spell is cast
on all her curses reach.

Take care to hide when the wild witch
    rides
to shriek her evil spell.
What she may do with a word or two
is much too grim to tell.

Jack Prelutsky

Witches

What does a witch look like to you? Is she old and very ugly with a long black cloak and pointed hat? Does she fly off on a broomstick and leave her black cat to watch over a spell cooking on a great pot on the fire? If so, then your idea of a witch is much the same as most people's.

Nowadays most of us associate wicked old witches with storybooks but, in the past, people thought that there was a witch in every town and village.

Very often some poor old woman, wizened and bent with age, might be thought of as a witch, and if a woman was unfortunate enough to be diseased or deformed she, too, ran the risk of being called one.

A witch might not always be an old person. People believed that it was possible for certain persons to have been born with evil powers, so sometimes quite young women came to be regarded as witches. And of course not all witches were women; some were men.

People's fear of witches

The witch was blamed for everything that went wrong in the village and people lived in fear of her powers. Her spells and curses were thought strong enough to make the crops fail and cause cattle to die. If people suffered disease or fell ill it was said to be due to the witch. Even small misfortunes or calamaties might be put down to her, such as the milk in the dairy going sour or a household being troubled by a plague of mice or rats.

Raising storms

Some witches were even held responsible for controlling the weather. It was believed they were able to call the wind, raise a storm, or start a drought.

Sailors and fishermen went in special dread of witches. They feared that if they displeased a witch, she might use her powers to send a storm violent enough to sink their ships.

A painful curse

There was one thing that a witch could do

that people dreaded most of all. This was to make a little image of a person in wax or clay and use it to inflict pain, sickness, or even death.

The power of the spell was strengthened if the witch could include in the model something that belonged to the person, such as a strand of hair, a nail clipping, or even mud from his shoes.

The spell began once the image was given the person's name. Then, when the model was touched, the victim would immediately feel it in that same part of his body.

Pins stuck in the model's limbs or head caused violent pains or madness. A pin stuck through the heart brought instant death.

If a clay figure was buried so that it would slowly disintegrate, or if a wax figure was allowed to melt, then the victim would die of a slow, wasting disease.

Of course, once a person imagined that such a frightful spell had been set to work against him, sheer terror was enough to make him suffer from imaginary and mysterious pains and illnesses.

A witch's most feared weapon was to practise sympathetic magic. This was done by injuring an object such as a doll or an effigy in the belief that the harm done would be transferred to the victim, who would suffer pain or even death. Here a sheep's heart and an effigy were found on the door of a ruined castle at Castle Rising.

Witch bottles, like this one, were widely believed to be the only sure way to remove a witch's spell. It was filled with the victim's urine, nail clippings, and some hair, as well as iron nails and the heart of an animal. Then it was heated to boiling point, causing the witch an agonizing and searing pain in her body.

A doll and a curse that was delivered to a victim by an evil-wisher.

The making of a witch

A woman would sometimes claim that she had become a witch after the Devil had appeared to her and persuaded or terrified her into giving her soul to him.

The Devil appeared in many forms: sometimes as a man dressed in black, sometimes as a black imp, or even as an animal such as a ferret or a goat.

To give herself to the Devil a woman would bend down with one hand on her head and the other under her feet. Then she would say:

'I give thee all that is between my hands.'

Then the Devil would bite her to leave a mark somewhere on her body. This bite was called the Devil's mark and it was a sure sign of being a witch.

Familiars

In order to help a witch to do his evil work, the Devil lent the witch a demon. This demon would be in the form of a small animal such as a cat, a weasel, or a rat.

The name of such an animal was a *familiar*. Witches were supposed to feed them with their own blood. If a woman was seen to have a wart or blemish somewhere on her body, it was considered to be the place from which she fed her familiar.

Witches' covens

Because they worked for the Devil, witches did not work alone. Each one belonged to a group of twelve witches called a coven. Every Friday night they would fly on their broomsticks to a meeting called a sabbat. In charge of the sabbat would be the Devil, or someone sent by him. The witches would call him Master.

At the sabbat the witches would talk about their evil doings and end up feasting and dancing.

At Hallowe'en all the covens would meet with their Grand Master, the Devil. On these nights people would take special care to protect themselves against passing witches. Doorways were hung with mistletoe, strings of garlic, and iron horseshoes, and people would take care to stay inside.

The witches' powers

Witches were said to fly to their sabbats. They usually went on broomsticks, but it was also claimed that they flew on cats, cockerels, and bundles of straw.

They were supposed to be able to fly after rubbing themselves with a special ointment known as 'flying ointment', which was made from a number of horrible ingredients such as bats' blood and baby's fat.

Witches were also thought to be able to change themselves into animals. Often they took the form of a cat, but they were most likely to change into a hare, probably because a hare is able to run extremely fast.

There are many stories told about witches doing this. One tale tells how a hare, chased by hounds, was bitten in the back leg before escaping and vanishing into a cottage. The hare was not seen again but lying in bed in the cottage was an old woman, gasping for breath and bleeding from a wound in her leg, just like the bite of a dog.

Keeping the witch away

People were so afraid of a witch's power that they would do things to protect themselves. For instance, when they passed an old woman in the street, they would spit. Then, if she was a witch, the spitting would keep away any bad luck the old woman might bring.

Thirteen made up a coven which met on a Friday. No wonder Friday 13 was thought to be unlucky.

It was also thought wise to pick up bits of metal or wire and pins if any were lying about. If a witch found them she might use them in a spell to do harm. Most bits of metal could be thrown over a person's shoulder. Then the witch could not put any evil power in them. But pins had always to be picked up and kept.

People were afraid of witches doing harm to their babies. To protect them, a knife would be put at the bottom of a baby's cot. This was thought to keep the witch's magic away.

People also hung round glass balls in their windows. These were called witch balls. They were supposed to distract the attention of a witch and absorb her magic.

White witches

Not all witches were bad. There was one sort to whom people went for help or advice if they were ill or in trouble. These were the white witches, or wisemen (known in some places as *cunning* men and women).

The wiseman was really a kind of witch doctor who used a variety of cures and charms to rid people of simple ailments and illnesses.

Ordinary people used to hold the white witches in high regard and they came to rely on them for all kinds of things. They would consult them when something was lost or stolen; they might even ask the wiseman to settle an argument or patch up a quarrel with a neighbour.

Protection from black witches

Most important of all, people went to the wiseman for protection against any evil magic or bad spells that might have been cast on them by black witches.

The true white witch did not meddle with black magic. But even so, people were afraid of their powers and took good care not to get on the wrong side of them, just in case.

Some white witches were believed to have the power to make a person completely immobile. There are many stories telling how a person who had done wrong, or who had displeased a wiseman, had been frozen to the spot unable to move until the wiseman had released the power of the spell.

Born the seventh son of a seventh son, Cunning Murrell was a white witch who made a good deal of money removing spells from people who had been cursed by black witches. He had a magic mirror for finding lost property, a telescope for looking through walls, and a copper charm to tell whether his clients were honest. He died in 1860.

48

Plants and herbs

Most wisemen had a considerable knowledge of the healing powers of certain plants and herbs, so their cures and remedies were often very effective. However, they also chanted special words or used secret rites when gathering or preparing their ingredients, and they believed that 'magic' was an important part of their work.

This special knowledge was very important and every white witch was anxious to teach her secrets to one other person before she died. Sometimes a dying witch would breathe into the mouth of her apprentice in the belief that this way the special powers would be passed on.

The mandrake plant was once thought to have highly magical properties. Its long forked root gave it the appearance of a demon and it was believed that when pulled from the ground, it gave a horrifying shriek. Any man hearing this would die, and so to uproot the plant a hungry dog would be tied to it and some meat placed nearby.

Witch hunts

For hundreds of years people shared a deep-rooted suspicion and terror of black witchcraft. This fear of evil and the supernatural was felt all over Europe. Not only were people afraid of witches, they went in dread of such things as fairies, goblins, werewolves, and vampires.

This fear and hatred of witchcraft led to the great witch hunts which took place between 1450 and 1750.

Those who were suspected of being witches were arrested and put on trial. Before the trial every effort was made to get a confession. In some countries the suspects were put to such terrible and painful torture that many of them would end up by confessing to anything even though they were completely innocent.

If a confession was not obtained, there were certain tests by which it was thought possible to tell if a person was a witch or not.

Every witch was supposed to have a Devil's mark somewhere on her body. Any little wart or blemish, found by the witch hunters, was thought to be evidence.

When such marks were found, they were pricked with a special pin. If no pain was felt or the wound did not bleed, this was taken as a sure sign that the person was a witch.

Between 1645 and 1646 a man called Matthew Hopkins was responsible for the deaths of some 400 people. Known as the Witchfinder General, Hopkins looked for marks or blemishes on a person's body which he claimed were Devil's marks. If such marks when jabbed by a needle, failed to bleed the victim was said to be a witch. Hopkins made a good deal of money from finding witches in this way. In this picture he is shown with two witches and their familiars.

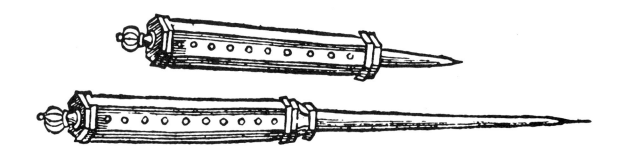

A way of proving if a woman was a witch was to prick her with a bodkin. If she didn't bleed she was thought to be guilty. This picture shows a genuine bodkin and a false one in which a spring loaded blade would retract into the handle.

Witch trials

No true witch was supposed to be able to say the Lord's Prayer. When on trial, many old women failed to do so. But this was not because they were witches. It was because they were frightened and confused, and the words simply would not come out.

The most popular of all witch tests was called swimming. The accused person was tied up with hands and feet bound cross-wise, the right hand tied to the left foot and vice versa. The victim was then flung into a pool or river in the belief that the water would reject her if she was guilty. Thus if she sank she was innocent, but if she floated it was a sure sign that she was a witch.

Superstitions about witches

Witches always stir in an anticlockwise direction. So always stir clockwise. To stir 'like a witch' is said to be extremely unlucky.

Do you crush the shell of your boiled egg, or push your spoon through the bottom when you've finished it? Then you are doing what superstitious people always did in the past, to stop witches collecting up the shells and floating them out to sea to cast a spell over fishermen and bring them bad luck.

In some parts of the county women still whistle when answering a knock on the door in case it is the Devil calling.

Ducking a witch.

Witch goes shopping

Witch rides off
Upon her broom,
Finds a space
To park it.
Takes a shiny shopping cart
Into the supermarket.
Smacks her lips and reads
The list of things she needs:
    'Six bats' wings,
    Worms in brine,
    Ears of toads,
    Eight or nine.
    Slugs and bugs,
    Snake skins dried,
    Buzzard innards,
    Pickled, fried.'
Witch takes herself
From shelf to shelf,
Cackling all the while,
Up and down and up and down and
In and out each aisle.
Out come cans and cartons
Tumbling to the floor.
'This,' says Witch, now all a-twitch
'Is a crazy store.
I CAN'T FIND A SINGLE THING
I AM LOOKING FOR!'

Lilian Moore

52

a witch's costume

You will need:

for the cone—a sheet of black card or sugar paper 45 cm × 35 cm (18″ × 14″)

for the brim—a sheet of black card 30 cm × 30 cm (12″ × 12″)

for the hair—string (sisal or polypropylene)

latex glue, sticky tape, scissors, pins or paper clips, black poster paint.

To make the hat

Use a rectangular piece of paper. 45 cm × 35 cm (18″ × 14″) is a good size but you can vary these dimensions. Draw a curve making the radius the width of the paper as shown in

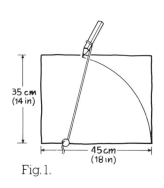

Fig. 1.

Draw a line from point A to point B as shown in Fig. 2 and cut off the shaded parts.

The area between A B & C is where you begin to roll your cone and this area, when rolled in, will help to strengthen the tip. Fig. 3. Before you stick the cone, place it on the head of the witch so that it fits snugly, not tightly. Pin together (or use paper clips) and test again on the head. Stick the cone using latex glue or sticky tape (remove any pins first).

For the brim, draw a circle from the bottom of the cone. If you press the two sides together you will make an oval shape and this will fit the head more accurately. Fig. 2.B

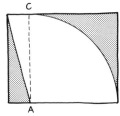

Fig. 2.

Draw a brim about 6.5 cm (2½″) wide, and then you should draw an additional strip on the inside of this, about 2.5 cm (1″) wide to make tabs for sticking to the cone.

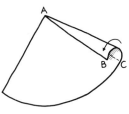

Fig. 3.

Cut out the brim, scoring the tabs and folding them upwards to be glued to the inside of the cone. Fig 4.

When dry, paint the brim with black poster paint.

To make the hair

Cut pieces of string to the required length, say 25.5 cm (10″) at the back, and 10 cm (4″) at the side. Unravel the string completely. Comb out so that it becomes fine, like hair. Stick inside the hat using the following

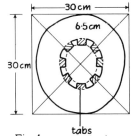

Fig. 4.

method: first lay out the string on a formica-surfaced table in two lines of short strands for the sides and two lines of long strands for the back. The string should be straight and tidy. Brush glue along these edges and round the inside of the brim. When both surfaces become tacky press them together carefully. Don't forget to leave a gap for the face!

The witchstone of Scrapfaggot Green

The county of Essex, on the outskirts of London, is known in history as 'The Witch County'. The reason for this is that from the middle of the sixteenth century to the end of the seventeenth, there were more 'witches' tried, tortured, and put to death in the area than anywhere else in the British Isles.

We know that many of these poor people were not witches at all, but harmless old men or women who had somehow upset their neighbours and thus been accused of being in league with the Devil. Some of them probably knew all about country cures and used their potions to help relieve minor illnesses at a time when there were no local doctors. But unfortunately when these cures worked, superstitious neighbours thought it was sure proof that they were aided by Satan himself. Anyone who was suspected of being a witch was for most of the time treated with awe and avoided at all costs. But when the authorities began to root out all those who were said to be enemies of the Church, accusing fingers would be raised. And it is a measure of the fear that people had of witches—whether they were real or not—that this fear often continued after the witch was dead.

Just off the A12 road between the towns of Chelmsford and Braintree lies the charm-ing little village of Great Leighs. The village has an impressive Norman church, two fine pubs, and a few shops. It also has a little area of common around a crossroads with the extraordinary name of Scrapfaggot Green. It is here that the story begins back in the year 1944 at the end of the Second World War.

The Americans had joined Britain, and all over England convoys of troops and weapons began to move up and down the roads, and even in the narrow lanes of Essex.

In the first week of June, a particularly large convoy of American tank-carriers passed through the village of Great Leighs. They were east-bound towards the coast from their depot and had already been on the road for almost two days. The weather was hot and close, and the drivers had lost patience with the crawling speed which was the best they could make along the narrow Essex lanes. Just as the leading driver was about to make a turn at the crossroads known as Scrapfaggot Green, he muttered a curse and slammed on his brakes. There was a large stone standing by the roadside, and he knew his load was too wide to get by it.

The American dropped from the cab of his truck and walked forward towards the stone, scratching his head. It was a huge, weathered piece of rock, standing all of eight feet high, and set firmly in the earth. On the top, it had a strange hole. Even at a quick estimate he reckoned it must weigh all of two tons. The man looked around. Even by pulling over to the far side of the road, he could not hope to squeeze by. It looked as if the convoy would have to turn round and find another route. But that would ruin their schedule. As the man stood thinking, a couple of other drivers from vehicles that had pulled up behind came to join him.

'Darned rock,' the first American muttered. 'We'll never clear it with these wide loads.'

One of the other drivers went over to the rock and slapped its smooth grey surface. 'Reckon we could shift it to one side? Don't seem to be doing too much here.'

The three Americans looked at each other for a moment. It would certainly save them going back—and surely the folk here wouldn't mind them moving the stone? Besides, there didn't seem to be anyone about.

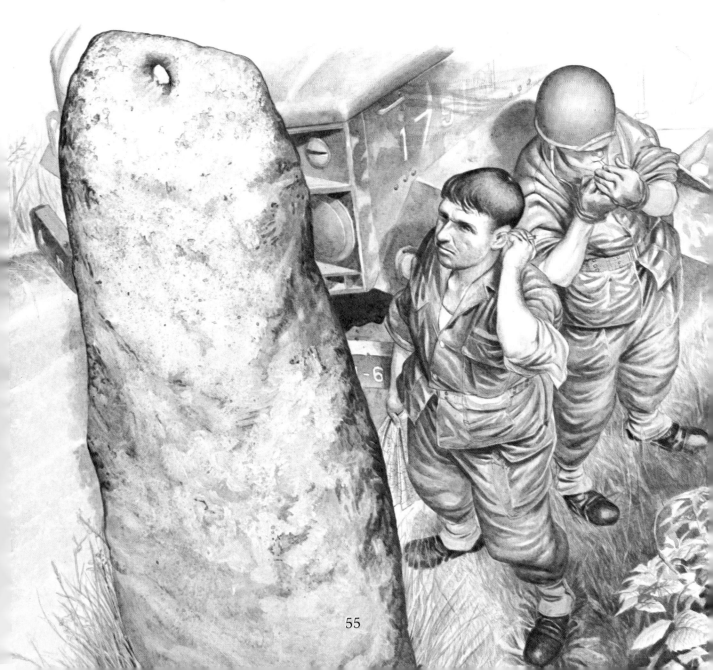

'Right. Let's shift it,' the first driver said, making up his mind. He moved quickly back to his cab. From inside he pulled out a steel hawser, and with the help of his two companions this was linked around the stone and joined up to the front bumper of the truck. Back in his cab again, the American applied full power to his truck and began easing backwards. The wire grew taut and for a moment the stone held firm. Increasing his accleration, the driver felt the wheels of his vehicle slip momentarily. Then, gradually, the stone began to lean over from its standing position. The man pressed his foot down harder and the stone eased out from its resting place. He pulled the rock several yards from its former position and then stopped once more. He released the steel hawser from the stone and the vehicle, and five minutes later all the trucks in the convoy successfully navigated the crossroads and disappeared into the distance.

For the best part of quarter of an hour the stone lay on its side in the sunshine until the first person walked by and saw what had happened. He was an old man, and it took him several moments to fully understand why *something* about the common looked different. When he realized what it was, he hurried off back to the village. There he burst into the public bar of the St. Anne's Castle Inn and announced in a voice that was almost shaking, 'Someone's moved the Witch's Stone.'

The group of old men who sat enjoying their first pints of beer of the day looked up with puzzled expressions.

'Moved it, George?' one of them said. 'Don't be daft. Thing's too heavy to move.'

'I tell you it's been shifted,' the man insisted. 'Over on its side, it is. Come and look if you don't believe me.'

Within the hour the story was flying around Great Leighs that the Witch's Stone on Scrapfaggot Green had indeed been removed. Probably something to do with the big convoy that had gone through earlier, one of the locals reckoned.

'No good will come of it,' an old woman muttered, shaking her head. She, for one, knew the sinister reputation of the stone which had stood at the crossroads for almost three hundred years. For underneath, it was said, was the body of a witch who had worked such evil in her life that the rock had been put over her grave to ensure she did not rise again to terrify the neighbourhood. To the younger people of Great Leighs such a story was just superstitious nonsense. For them the stone was something for children to play on, or courting couples to sit beside.

But over the next few days they were to be made to eat their words. Because within hours of the stone being moved, the village was terrorized by a series of events that are quite unique in supernatural lore.

The incidents began the following night. In the early hours of the morning the bell in the church tower began to chime all of its own accord. And then at 2.30 a.m. the clock on the steeple struck midnight, the twelve chimes ringing eerily out across the village, waking several of its inhabitants. For many nights thereafter the clock was to do exactly the same thing.

In Great Leighs next morning, several people were surprised to find that none of their hens had laid any eggs. And a number of others discovered some of their chickens missing. They later recovered these—all drowned in water butts.

Nor did the strange reports end there. Ernest Withen at Chadwicks Farm awoke to find that the stacks he had built only a few days previously were broken down and spread all over his yard. Yet he knew there had been no strong wind during the night. He was even more puzzled by the fact that all his hay wagons had been moved from the places in which he had left them in his sheds. On another farm, the owner also found some of his haystacks pushed over, and a group of stacks moved from one field to another. A shepherd named Alf Quilter, going to tend his flock, found that half were in their pen, and half out of it—although the hurdle was still closed and the surrounding fence was not damaged in any way. In the local builder's yard belonging to Charlie Dickson, piles of heavy scaffolding poles which normally took strong, fit men to shift them were scattered about the ground like so many matchsticks.

By the mid-morning of the day after the moving of the stone, it was clear that almost everyone in the village had some uncanny story to report. But it was only one or two of the very old people who thought it might have anything to do with the stone. The next night brought another fresh crop of mysterious happenings. Arthur Sykes, the landlord of the St. Anne's Castle Inn, found three geese missing without a trace, and admitted uneasily that during the night furniture had been moved about his premises, seemingly by invisible hands. In one of the bedrooms a chest of drawers had been tipped over, a heavy wardrobe moved across the room, and the bedclothes torn from the bed and strewn about the floor. Bill Reynolds, the landlord of the other pub, the Dog and Gun, had been jovially sceptical of all the stories after the first night. People's imagination playing tricks on them, was his verdict. The next morning he woke up to find a heavy stone that he had never seen before blocking his front door.

Within three days, the story reached the newspapers and made front page news across the country. The reporters who descended on Great Leighs found no evidence of a hoax, and no shortage of new outbreaks to report. But now, they seemed to be getting more dangerous.

Thirty sheep and two horses were found dead in a field, and the disturbances in the bedroom at the St. Anne's Castle Inn were repeated again with still more violent upheaval—leaving Arthur Sykes even more bewildered than before. As he told a friend later, 'I just don't understand it. From the way the room was upset I should certainly have heard something going on. I was sleeping in the next bedroom. But I never heard a thing.'

Mr Sykes had an even stranger experience to recount to one of the newspaper reporters. 'It happened out in the street—in broad daylight. I saw this cut-throat razor lying on the ground. I went to pick it up—and it jumped clean away from me. I tried the same thing again and once more it jumped away from me. It couldn't have been a joke—someone pulling it with a piece of thread. For you see it kept jumping up and down, each time about a foot into the air. Frankly it frightened me, so I just left it there and went away.'

By now the village was also being investigated by a psychic expert who soon confessed himself just as baffled as the locals. He could find no evidence at all that human agency was involved in any of the incidents.

In the public bar of the St. Anne's Castle, the conviction really began to grow that somehow the mysterious events might all be connected with the moving of the stone.

The men in the bar had all heard the whisper going round the village that it was the witch who was responsible. That by removing the stone, her ghost had been set free and was now wreaking her vengence on the village. At first hearing, such talk sounded as if it had come straight from the superstitious Middle Ages. But when modern science was baffled by such events—and it was—perhaps it would be as well to take a little bit of notice of it.

'I reckon we should put the stone back where it was.' The old man who now spoke had been silent for some time as he listened to the arguments going backwards and forwards in the bar. 'Would do no harm, would it? And if things still went on happening it might put an end to the stories about the witch.'

It was an idea that had occurred to several of the others, but they had been a bit reluctant to suggest it. It seemed somehow to be giving in to superstition. For a short while, the little group talked about it. They knew the stone was heavy, but if one of them got a tractor they could surely drag it back into its old position by the road? Yes, that was what they would do. At the worst it would tidy up the common again, and at best, well...

Later that same evening a group of the men drove out to Scrapfaggot Green on a tractor and successfully hauled the stone back into its slot. It went in easily, one of the men remembered, almost smoothly. In the silence and darkness of night they worked, the men could almost swear they heard a rustling in the undergrowth and then a groan as the massive grey rock dropped back into place. But that could have been just the eeriness of the situation.

What is for sure, though, is that Great Leighs has not been disturbed again from that moment, and if it was the ghost of the old witch who the Americans unknowingly released, then she has lain quietly ever since. But today, you will not find anyone in that pretty little village who will consider for a moment any suggestion that the rock on Scrapfaggot Green should be moved again...

Peter Haining

At the foot of an oak tree, outside the gate of a small square-towered church in the village of Shebbear in North Devon stands a huge, flat, reddish-coloured rock. The rock is said to have been thrown there by the Devil.

Every year on 5 November, a group of local people gather outside the village public house with a collection of poles and crowbars. Having fortified themselves with a pint of good ale they go to the rock and turn it over. The men of the village have been doing this for hundreds of years in order to bring good luck and prosperity to the village.

A coven of witches usually consists of 13 witches.

This coven is playing the ancient game of pass the toad.

Witch Facts?

A favourite spell of witches and wizards is to turn a Prince into a frog, or Rover into a toad.

If you want to know the way ask an old witch.

Witches have been known to live to a great age some well beyond 65 years.

An old witch in her later years will teach all she knows to a young novice

Many witches practise great skill in the art of broomstick flying.

In ancient times both male and female witches were often said to have the ability to worry sheep.

another worried sheep.

Ⅽ Two worried sheep.

Witches are very fond of cats, especially black cats. They are the most popular choice as familiars and, like witches, have long been misunderstood.

Twins especially witch twins, have long been thought to possess unique powers. Although also regarded by many to be double trouble.

HOW TO PERFORM

witch Widdershin's magic tricks

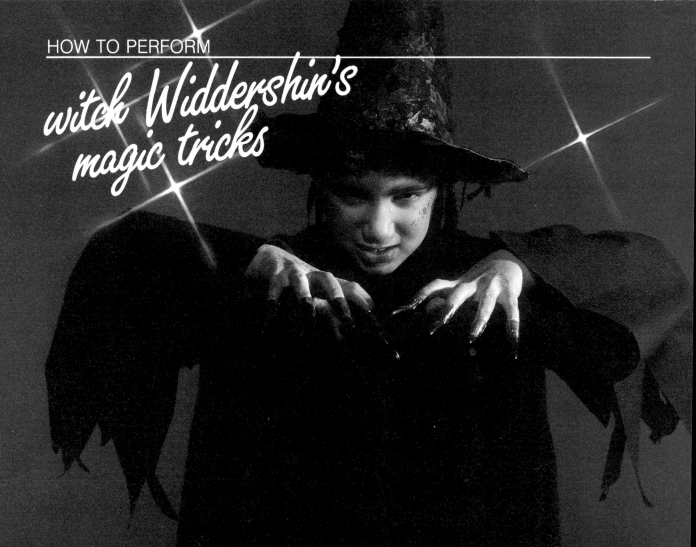

You might like to try performing a few conjuring tricks at your party. What better place to try some magic than in your spooky party room with its dim lighting and weird atmosphere!

If you do try some conjuring tricks, be sure to practise them beforehand until you can do them really well. Even simple tricks will not go smoothly at first, and you may need to do them several times over before you can perform them in front of other people.

As soon as you can work with confidence you will stand a better chance of fooling your audience. All good magicians put on an act and you, too, will

be wise to work out what to say and how to present each trick well in advance.

The tricks shown here are just a few examples of things you can prepare without a great deal of effort. You may, of course, have some tricks of your own that you can do, such as card tricks. Whatever happens be sure to do tricks you can do with ease.

A word of warning: some of the tricks on these pages use matchsticks. Matches can be dangerous so ask a grown-up to give you safety matches with their heads cut off. Never take matches without permission.

The magic string

'Witch Widdershins had enchanted teeth. She could chew two bits of string together and make them into one. This is what she did.'

Hold up two pieces of string. Put the upper ends in your mouth and let the lower ends hang down. Then chew the string, making faces and rolling your eyes. When you pull on one end of the string it comes out in one whole piece.

Here's how it's done

You use one long piece of string which you fold in half so that both ends hang down.

Loop it on to a short piece of string, so that the ends of the short piece stick up. Fig. 2. Hide the loop with your thumb. Fig. 2.

Put the loop in your mouth and hold the short ends with your teeth. Fig. 3.

Pull out the long piece (use both hands if you need to).

The amazing safety-pin

For your next trick you can say:

'Here is Witch Widdershins' amazing safety-pin. It has a mind of its own. It can do itself up all by itself. Watch this.'

You undo the safety-pin and lay it on the table. Then you show the audience both sides of a small square of cloth, before laying it over the pin. Say a magic word and snatch the cloth away. Hey presto! The pin has fastened itself up.

How it's done

Tie a piece of black cotton to the pin that you show to the audience. Fix the other end of the cotton to your sleeve just below your elbow. (If you have a black cloth on the table, the cotton won't be seen.)

Pick up a fastened safety-pin secretly with your left hand, at the same time as you pick up the cloth. (Don't use your right hand too much in case you jerk the cotton.)

As you place the cloth on the table, drop the concealed pin next to the unfastened one. Jerk your elbow away so that the unfastened pin flies off the table while hidden by the cloth.

Practise a way to snap the cotton secretly to get rid of the safety-pin that is hanging from the thread on your elbow.

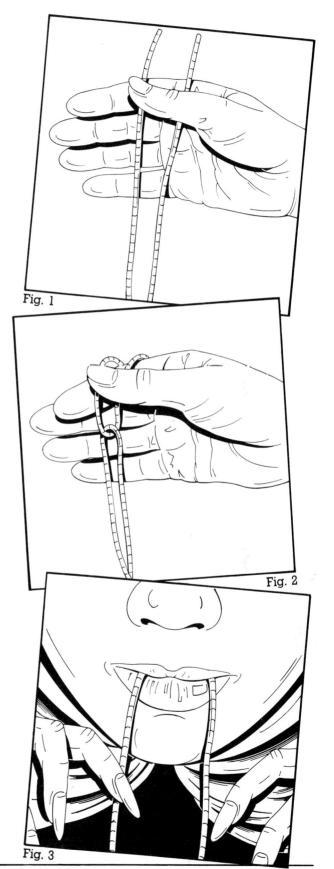

Fig. 1

Fig. 2

Fig. 3

Watch the match

Now you can say:

'Witch Widdershins' safety-pin is so magical that a match can pass clean through it. Watch this.'

You hold the safety-pin between the thumb and first finger of your left hand. Behind it you hold a match. A moment later the match appears to pass through the safety-pin.

How it's done

Hold a safety-pin between the thumb and forefinger of the left hand. Hold the match a little differently. Grip it between the first and second fingers (Fig. 1) and rest the thumb lightly on the other end.

Fig. 1

Fig. 2

Don't move the left hand. All the action is in the right. As you pull the match towards the pin, move the thumb away slightly from the end of the match. Fig. 2. The match will slide round the pin and flick back into position under your thumb. It will happen so fast that your audience won't see how it happens, but it will look just as though the match has passed through the pin.

The amazing match

Go on to say:

'I suppose you think there's some trick, getting a matchstick to pass through the magic safety-pin. Well I'll prove just how amazing this safety-pin is.'

You open the safety-pin and push the point of the pin through the centre of the match. Shut the pin again then hold one end of it firmly. Say, 'Now watch the match pass through the solid steel bar of the pin.'

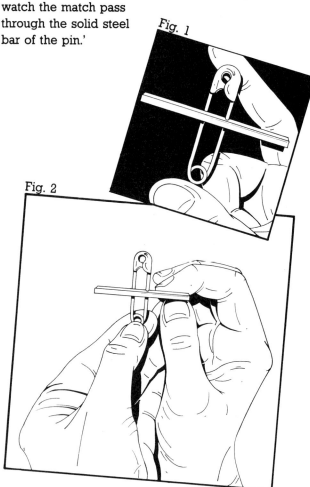

Fig. 1

Fig. 2

Make sure that the left half of the stick is in front of the bar of the pin. Fig. 1

Use the edge of your right thumb nail to tweak the matchstick. To everyone's amazement the left half of the stick appears on the other side of the bar. Fig. 2

How it's done

When you flick the end of the match it spins around and ends up in front of the bar. The action is so rapid that no one—not even you will see it happen.

However, practise the best way to flick the end of the match with your nail. Learn how hard to flick it, so that the match pivots round at just the right speed.

(The match will be less likely to split if you soak it in water for a minute or two before pushing the pin through.)

The magic cotton reel

Show the audience a black cloth bag and take out from it three cotton reels or thread spools, one of which has two pieces of string running through the hole in the centre.

Say: '**This is Witch Widdershins' magic cotton reel. It keeps disappearing, so that's why I've tied it up, because I don't want it to vanish this time.**'

Begin to tie a knot, as in Fig. 1.

'**Look, I'll just make sure it can't get away by tying a knot in the string.**'

Now you show the audience the ordinary black bag, then put the cotton reels in, leaving the bewitched reel until last. Now the bag stands on the table with the string from the bewitched reel sticking from the top. Say:

'**Now let's see if that wretched reel has fooled me.**'

You empty the bag. There are only two reels inside. You pull out the loops of string with no cotton reel on them!

How it's done

Prepare two pieces of string, tying them with fine black cotton or thread. Cut the ends of the cotton so that only a small circle is left. Now pass the string through the reel so that the ring join is concealed inside. Fig. 2

Make the black bag with a slit in the bottom near one corner. The audience will not notice this, if you hold the slit as you show them the inside of the bag.

As you place the bewitched reel in the bag, poke your fingers through the slit, and hold the reel. Hold the strings firmly and pull the reel sharply enough to snap the cotton-ring. Fig. 3

Conceal the reel, and practise a way to dispose of it before opening the bag again.

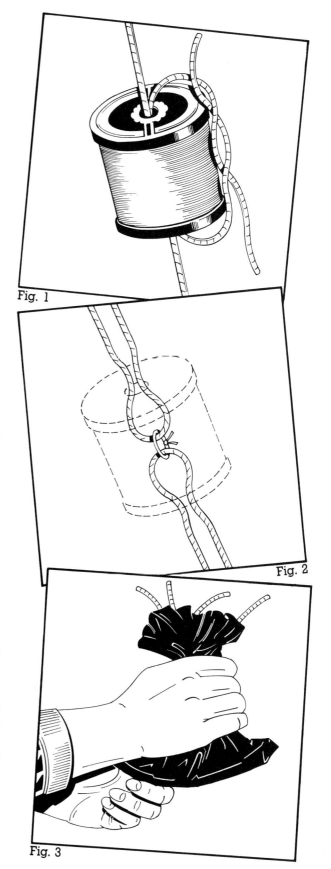

Fig. 1

Fig. 2

Fig. 3

The Salem witch trials

In 1692, the parents of a number of girls at Salem Village in Massachusetts, USA, were alarmed when their daughters began to suffer from the symptoms of a frightening disorder.

The girls would be seized by fits in which their bodies would jerk violently, or be twisted into strange and unnatural shapes. During these fits it took an enormous amount of physical strength from adults to hold the girls still or straighten their rigid bodies and bent limbs.

At other times the girls experienced terrifying hallucinations in which they claimed that they were tormented by weird spectres who pinched and bit them; indeed there were often marks and bruises to be found on the girls' bodies. Such terrors left them temporarily unable to speak, hear, or see.

The girls were suffering from a condition known to doctors today as hysteria. This sometimes happens when a group of people are so badly affected by fear or nervousness that, all at the same time, they feel ill or faint, or suffer from fits. As often happens in cases of group hysteria, the Salem girls were affecting each other. Each time one of them became hysterical she would trigger off the others.

Two of the girls, Elizabeth Parris, aged 9 and Abigail Williams, 11, were the daughter and niece of the Reverend Samuel Parris, a minister at Salem. Extremely worried, Revd Parris asked the advice of men who had studied medicine, one of whom came to the conclusion that the girls were bewitched. They were, he said, the victims of a spiteful and vicious sort of evil deliberately brought about by someone.

Revd Parris did not want to think that there were witches in his community. Had the girls somehow disturbed the forces of evil by tampering with the occult? He found out that one of the older girls in the group had tried to tell her own fortune by gazing into the white of an egg placed in a rounded glass. And there she had seen a coffin. This threw her into a state of shock and terror.

It emerged that the girls had been helped in their occult experiments by Parris's own servant, a woman called Tituba. Her lurid stories of ghosts, demons, and the supernatural had overexcited the girls' vivid imaginations and sent them into a turmoil of nervousness.

This engraving shows Tituba telling some of the girls one of her terrifying tales.

Nowadays, with our knowledge of medicine and psychology it is hard to imagine why the parents could not put an end to the girls' hysterical behaviour. But it must be remembered that, in those days, people believed very strongly in the power of the supernatural. For over a hundred years people in Europe lived in the fear of witchcraft, and tens of thousands had been hunted down, brought to trial, and executed.

It is hardly surprising, therefore, that the devout, God-fearing Puritans of New England should have shared this dread of witches and have held a deeply rooted belief in the Devil and all his works.

Matters came to a head when one of the girls' aunts baked a witch-cake. This cake, made from barley meal mixed with the girls' urine, was given to a dog in the belief that the evil which possessed the girls would then pass into the dog.

Parris was shocked and angry. He believed in the power of prayer. The witch-cake he considered to be a dangerous spell. 'The Devil has been raised among us,' he announced, '... and when he shall be silenced the Lord only knows.'

His words started a horrifying chapter in the history of witch-hunts, and the girls became the cause of a tragic drama which was to cost the lives of twenty people. What had begun as a genuine hysteria developed into a frightening sort of game which the girls became unable to control.

The moment that people thought witch-craft was involved, the eyes of the whole community were focused on the girls. They began, secretly, to delight in the sensation they were causing. They started to play up to the adults' fears and to behave in such a way that made sure they were the centre of attention.

As well as Elizabeth Parris and Abigail Williams, there were also Ann Putnam 12, Mary Walcott 16, Elizabeth Hubbard 17, Susan Sheldon and Elizabeth Booth, both 18, Mercy Lewis 19, and Elizabeth Proctor 20. As events unfolded, the girls were joined by other impressionable girls, most of them in their late teens.

The question was asked: who had bewitched them? The girls named two simple-minded women, Sarah Osburn and Sarah Good. They also named Tituba.

At the hearing before magistrates, Sarah Good, charged with being a witch, strongly denied that she was in league with the Devil or had done the girls any harm. But the girls, who were at the hearing, took their cue from each other and fell into a fit, claiming that Sarah Good's spirit had left her body and was attacking them by biting and pinching.

Tituba provided the magistrates with an astonishing confession. She had, she said, given herself to the Devil and had signed his book in which were the names of nine other witches.

Her confession was pure fantasy. She alleged that she had ridden on a pole with Sarah Good, Sarah Osburn, and two other witches. They had flown above the rooftops and she had been forced to go with them to torment the girls. Salem was driven into a turmoil of fear and suspicion. People threw sideways glances at each other; Tituba's confession had mentioned nine other witches—who were they?

One of the girls, Ann Putnam, then accused a fourth woman called Martha Corey. Martha was a respectable woman who hotly denied the charges made against her. In her agitated state at the hearing, she wrung her hands and bit her lip. At once several girls complained that they had been bitten and pinched. 'Look,' they cried. 'She is doing it to us now.'

All the women, except Tituba, were committed for trial. Amazingly, those who confessed to being witches were not condemned to death, nor indeed sent for trial. It was only those who denied witchcraft and protested their innocence who were tried and executed. Tituba was reprieved, but remained in gaol.

During the months that followed, Salem was gripped by witch-hunt madness. The victims of this madness ranged from the most respected and well-to-do members of the community to the poorest and most humble.

Often, after the girls had named a person, spiteful or wrong-minded people would come forward with lies or ridiculous evidence which in normal times would have been laughed at.

Throughout the trials the magistrates accepted as their main evidence the testimony of the girls, who continued to claim that the spirits of the accused had physically attacked and hurt them.

For example, Elizabeth Proctor made this sworn statement, 'That I have been most grievously tormented by my neighbour, John Proctor, or his appearance (spirit). Also I have seen his appearance most grievously torment and afflict Mary Walcott, Mercy Lewis, and Ann Putnam by pinching, twisting, and choking them.'

On the basis of this, John Proctor was later convicted of witchcraft and hanged.

The magistrates were even convinced when the girls' fits were brought on by the presence of a complete stranger. They accepted as evidence the 'touch test'. If the girls in a fit were quietened by a person's touch, that person was sure to be guilty, the evil having been passed back into him.

Over 150 people were arrested during the period of madness at Salem. Of these, thirty-one (six of whom were men) were sentenced to death. Nineteen of these unfortunate people were hanged and two died in gaol. One was pressed to death by heavy weights: an ancient form of execution for anyone refusing to plead either guilty or not guilty.

The Salem witch hunt was no more terrible than many of those which took place in Europe between 1450 and 1750, in which 100,000 people were put to death. That people should have been so blinded by fear and superstition, as so many were at Salem in 1692, shows the extraordinary way that people's minds were gripped by a belief in the Devil and the powers of evil.

Nevertheless, the horrors at Salem were recognized by a number of people at the time, many of whom suspected that the girls were only pretending to have fits and were lying about their hallucinations.

In later years, several of those involved in the terrible events made statements saying that they had been wrong in what they said at the trials. In admitting that they had been mistaken, or had given false evidence, they claimed to have acted without fully understanding what they were doing.

This was probably true. Only by looking back at themselves could people fully realize the folly of what had happened and see for themselves that the witch hunts were the result of a delusion.

Fantasy

I think if I should wait some night in an
  enchanted forest
With tall dim hemlocks and moss-
  covered branches,
And quiet, shadowy aisles between the
  tall blue-lichened trees;
With low shrubs forming grotesque
  outlines in the moonlight,
And the ground covered with a thick
  carpet of pine needles
So that my footsteps made no sound,—

They would not be afraid to glide
  silently from their hiding places
To the white patch of moonlight on the
  pine needles,
And dance to the moon and the stars and
  the wind.

Their arms would gleam white in the
  moonlight
And a thousand dewdrops sparkle in the
  dimness of their hair;
But I should not dare to look at their
  wildly beautiful faces.

Ruth Mather Skidmore

The fairy folk

Hallowe'en will come, will come,
Witchcraft will be set a-going.
Fairies will be at full speed
Running in every pass.
Avoid the road children, children.

Traditional children's song

As if witches, demons and ghosts were not enough to contend with, our ancestors also faced another danger, especially at Hallowe'en. This was the malice of goblins, elves, pixies, and a host of other evil or mischievous sprites.

As big as humans

Nowadays we think of fairies as tiny, gentle winged creatures, who spend much of their time dancing and sporting in flowery glades or ferny glens, and who have certain magical powers. Sometimes a fairy might use these powers to help a person who has done them a kindness, or sometimes they might use them to help a person in trouble.

In the past, however, people did not hold such a romantic view of them. They believed in many different kinds of fairies, some of whom were as big as human beings, were spiteful, and were hideously ugly. Even the kindest sort of fairy was thought to be dangerous.

It was widely thought that some fairies were anxious to steal human babies and replace them with a 'changeling'—a baby of their own that was ugly and misshapen.

Dangers

It was also well known that certain fairies were fond of playing unpleasant tricks on people, such as stealing food or certain possessions, milking cows in the fields, causing the fire not to burn, or turning the milk sour, and so on.

Another danger, especially at times of the year such as Hallowe'en, was that an unlucky person might come across a band of

These elfin-like babies are changelings, left by the fairies in exchange for human babies.

fairy folk and be so enchanted by their music and dancing that he would join in. While the fairy dance was going on for what seemed like only a few minutes to the human, months, or even years, of ordinary time would pass. Finally the person would return to his loved ones to find they had grown old, or had died, in his absence.

The following story shows the sort of thing that could happen to the unwary traveller after dark:

Two young men were coming home after nightfall on Hallowe'en, each with a jar of whisky on his back. Suddenly they saw, as they thought, a house all lit up by the roadside, and from the house there came the sounds of music and dancing. In fact, it was not a house at all but a fairy knoll, and it was the fairies who were jigging about there so merrily.

One of the young men was deceived. He stepped into the house and joined in the dance, without even stopping to put down

the jar of whisky. His companion was wiser and suspected that the place was not what it seemed. When he entered, he took the precaution of sticking a needle in the door. That disarmed the power of the fairies, and so he got safely away.

On the same day a year later, he passed the same spot and what should he see but his poor friend still dancing away with the jar of whisky on his back. A weary man he was to be sure, but he begged to be allowed to finish the reel which he was dancing. But when they took him out into the open air, there was nothing left of him but skin and bones.

The fairy folk

The fairies in that story were those who belong to a group that people think of as 'fairy folk'. Such fairies live in 'fairyland'

under the ground or inside hills.

Fairyland is thought to be ruled by a queen, although sometimes there may be a king, too. In appearance these fairies look very much like humans and some may be extremely beautiful. They enjoy feasting and they spend their time dancing and singing.

Sometimes a fairy will come out of fairyland to mix with mortals, and there are stories of humans falling in love with fairy people, and even marrying them—often with unhappy consequences for the human.

The fairies keep horses and dogs. On certain nights they ride out on their white horses whose manes are braided and hung with silver bells, so that they tinkle as they move along. The fairy queen leads the procession, while the dogs run alongside the fairy band.

Household fairies

The household fairies are known as hobgoblins. They are called this because they sleep near the hearth (or hob), and come and go by way of the chimney.

Like his cousin the goblin (who is extremely unpleasant) the friendly hobgoblin is small, misshapen, and very ugly with a shaggy body. Usually he goes naked but sometimes he wears ragged clothes. He can make himself invisible at will and is only seen on occasions by the householder.

Although the hobgoblin will work hard in the house, he will be upset if anyone attempts to spy on him or catch him at his work, and he will be offended if anyone tries to offer him a reward. All the hobgoblin seeks is a bowl of milk and some bread left out at night. Woe betide the person who tries to give him anything more, for almost every hobgoblin who has been offered a suit of new clothes has left the house at once, never to come back.

The Hobgoblin laughed till his sides ached

Boggarts and other things

The second kind of fairies are quite different from fairy folk. They belong to a group which includes such beings as pixies, boggarts, brownies, dwarfs, elves, hobgoblins, selkies, and leprechauns.

These fairies live either alone or in small groups. Some of them inhabit places such as marshes, rivers, and woods; others live in houses where they are generally helpful even if, from time to time, they play mischievous tricks on the people in the house.

Other fairies of the second kind are those who do certain jobs such as shoemaking, blacksmithing, tin-mining, and so on. Very often they need help from human hands: for example, when they are unable to mend something, like an axe. A person who helps them out will always be well rewarded.

Who were the fairies?

It is hardly surprising that our ancestors should believe in fairies. In far-off days there were vast areas of forest, marsh-land, heath and hill country that were wild and untrodden. To travel anywhere was a lonely and dangerous undertaking. There were no roads—only tracks and footpaths.

After the hours of darkness, all the traveller had to guide him on moonless nights was the dim glow of a candle or a rush lantern.

Anyone out and about would need steely nerves as he encountered wraith-like mists in woodland and thicket, the weird light that flickered from burning marsh-gases, the strange phosphorescence that glowed over pools of stagnant water, and the peculiar clouds of powder that puffed up from fungi on rotted tree trunks.

One popular belief was that fairies were the ghosts or spirits of those who had died before Christianity came to Britain, or that they were the spirits of babies who had died before they had been baptized.

Another belief was that fairies were angels who had been driven out of heaven but were not wicked enough to live in Hell. It was thought by many that the fairies were obliged to make a payment each year to the Devil by sending some of their number to Hell. It was thought that this was the reason why the fairies would steal human babies or bewitch people to carry them off to fairyland.

Ancient Britons

One interesting explanation about the existence of fairies in Britain may, perhaps, be traced back to the time when the Celts invaded Britain in about 300 BC. The original inhabitants were driven into remote regions, where many of them lived in caves and underground caverns.

These small dark people may have been extremely shy and timid, but they were skilled at hiding in woods and forests. They moved by stealth, so that they were seen only rarely and then only at a glimpse. Occasionally one of them might cautiously accept a small gift of food in return for doing a task. Otherwise, these little people lived remote and hidden lives.

The Cottingly fairies

Mr Wright handed his thirteen-year-old daughter Elsie a camera and showed her how to use it. 'The next time you see some fairies, you can take their picture!' Mr Wright smiled to himself and sat down with the newspaper. Well, he had to stop Elsie somehow. He was tired of hearing her say she had seen fairies at the bottom of their garden.

It was not the end of the matter. Elsie and her 10-year-old cousin Frances went off and took a photograph. When it was developed Mr Wright was astonished to see a picture of Frances with a band of tiny dancing winged fairies.

Elsie and Frances insisted that the figures were real fairies. They had often seen them playing in the little glen at the back of their home at Cottingly near Bradford in Yorkshire.

Mr and Mrs Wright were puzzled. Had the girls faked the photographs—perhaps by using paper figures cut from a book? Both girls denied that the pictures were a trick, and a month later produced a second photograph, this time of a gnome about to hop on to Elsie's hand.

The photographs were put away and forgotten until three years later, in 1920, when Mrs Wright happened to show them

The first picture taken in 1917 showing 10-year-old Frances Griffiths with a group of dancing fairies.

The second picture was taken by Frances just as a pointed-faced gnome with a set of pipes on his back was about to hop on to Elsie's hand.

The fairy figures in Princess Mary's Gift Book on which the girls based their cut-outs.

to a psychic researcher called Edward Gardner.

Uncertain if the photographs were genuine, Gardner showed them to photographic experts, who were amazed by them. One said: 'These are entirely genuine unfaked photographs. There is no trace whatever of studio work involving paper models or painted figures.' Another expert thought they could have been faked, but only by a first-class photographer.

The girls were asked to take more photographs. This time the film was carefully marked by the manufacturer and the camera was checked and sealed.

Elsie and Frances came up with three pictures: one showed Frances with a leaping fairy; a second showed Elsie being offered a posy of flowers by a fairy; and the third was of a group of fairies dancing in the sun.

Edward Gardner was amazed by the quality of the pictures. If the girls were setting up tiny figures and photographing them, then they were extremely skilled.

An article about the girls and all the pictures was published in the 1920 Christmas edition of Strand Magazine. There was a tremendous reaction from people, some who cried 'Fake' and others who wrote to

say that they too had seen fairies just like the ones in the pictures.

Elsie and Frances took no more photographs but they stuck to their story that the pictures were a true likeness of their visitors.

In 1983, sixty-five years after the pictures had been taken, Elsie Wright finally admitted that the pictures were not of real fairies, but were set up by the girls using cut-out figures they had drawn themselves.

The figures were based on some drawings of fairies that they had seen in a book called 'Princess Mary's Gift Book.'

In making her admission, Elsie claimed that the pictures were taken because Frances had fallen in the brook and got into trouble. As her excuse, Frances said that she had been playing with fairies at the time. When the grown-ups refused to believe this, Elsie and Frances decided to prove that fairies did exist in the dell.

For Elsie and Frances, what was really a practical joke misfired. The reaction of such famous people as Sir Conan Doyle towards the pictures was such that the girls felt unable to own up, even if they had wanted to.

A luck

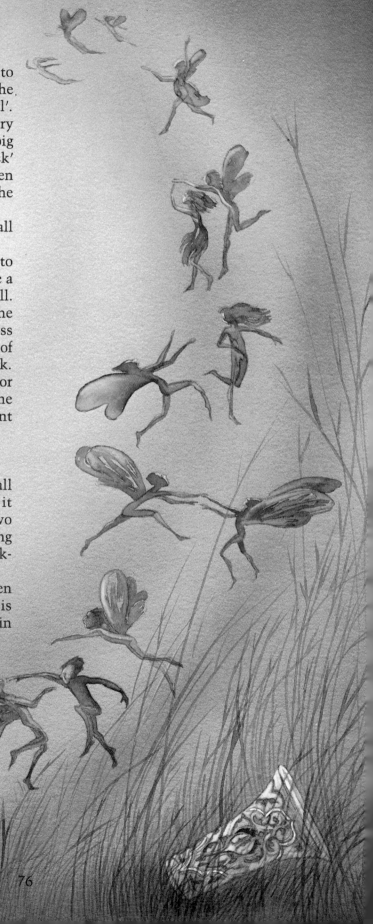

This beautiful green glass goblet is said to have once belonged to the fairies. The goblet is known as the 'Luck of Eden Hall'.

Eden Hall was once a large country house in Cumberland. In the past many big houses had objects called 'lucks'. A 'luck' had to be kept safely. If it was lost or broken it would mean that disaster would befall the house or its owner.

The story about the 'luck' of Eden Hall goes like this:

Long, long ago the butler was going to draw some water and was surprised to see a band of fairies dancing round the well. There, lying unguarded on the edge of the fairy circle, was a curiously painted glass goblet. The butler seized it, and, in spite of the fairies' protests, would not give it back.

Finding the butler more than a match for them, the fairies vanished, leaving the goblet in his possession. But as they went the fairy leader cried out:

'If that glass either break or fall,
Farewell the luck of Eden Hall.'

The goblet was kept safely at Eden Hall for hundreds of years. Only once did it become close to being broken: about two hundred years ago a guest at a drinking party accidently dropped it. Luckily a quick-witted servant caught it just in time.

The luck lasted until 1934 when Eden Hall was demolished. Today the goblet is kept in the Victoria and Albert Museum in London.

THE NIGHT

The bird of the night

A shadow is floating through the
    moonlight.
Its wings don't make a sound.
Its claws are long, its beak is bright.
Its eyes try all the corners of the night.

It calls and calls: all the air swells and
    heaves
And washes up and down like water.
The ear that listens to the owl believes
In death. The bat beneath the eaves.

The mice beneath the stone are still as
    death.
The owl's air washes them like water.
The owl goes back and forth inside the
    night,
And the night holds its breath.

Randall Jarrell

Colonel Fazackerley

1   Colonel Fazackerley Butterworth-
     Toast
    Bought an old castle complete with a
     ghost,
    But someone or other forgot to declare
    To Colonel Fazack that the spectre
     was there.

2   On the very first evening, while
     waiting to dine,
    The Colonel was taking a fine sherry
     wine,
    When the ghost, with a furious flash
     and a flare,
    Shot out of the chimney and shivered,
     'Beware!'

3   Colonel Fazackerley put down his
     glass
    And said, 'My dear fellow, that's really
     first class!
    I just can't conceive how you do it at
     all.
    I imagine you're going to a Fancy
     Dress Ball?'

4   At this, the dread ghost gave a
     withering cry.
    Said the Colonel (his monocle firm in
     his eye),
    'Now just how you do it I wish I could
     think.
    Do sit down and tell me, and please
     have a drink.'

5   The ghost in his phosphorous cloak
     gave a roar
    And floated about between ceiling and
     floor.
    He walked through a wall and
     returned through a pane
    And backed up the chimney and came
     down again.

6   Said the Colonel, 'With laughter I'm
     feeling quite weak!'
    (As trickles of merriment ran down his
     cheek.)
    'My house-warming party I hope you
     won't spurn.
    You *must* say you'll come and you'll
     give us a turn!'

7   At this, the poor spectre—quite out of
     his wits—
    Proceeded to shake himself almost to
     bits.
    He rattled his chains and he clattered
     his bones
    And he filled the whole castle with
     mumbles and moans.

8   But Colonel Fazackerley, just as
     before,
    Was simply delighted and called out,
     'Encore!'
    At which the ghost vanished, his
     efforts in vain,
    And never was seen at the castle again.

9   'Oh dear, what a pity!' said Colonel
     Fazack.
    'I don't know his name, so I can't call
     him back.'
    And then with a smile that was hard to
     define,
    Colonel Fazackerley went in to dine.

Werewolves

The wolf

The wolf is a creature that has always been hated and feared. A male wolf can grow to over two metres in length, including its powerful bushy tail, and it may weigh as much as 60 kilos. Because of its fearlessness and ferocious strength it can easily bring down a large animal such as a horse or a bison. A defenceless person is an easy prey for it.

As a killer of sheep and cattle, the wolf has always been man's natural enemy especially in the hungry months of winter. It is little wonder that the Anglo-Saxons called January the 'Wolf-Month'.

Wolves are still found in North America, Northern Asia, and in parts of Europe. Their blood-curdling howls send shivers down the spine of the most hardened person. It is not surprising that stories of werewolves are among the most frightening and gruesome of any to do with the supernatural.

The werewolf

The word werewolf means *man-wolf* and it was believed that a person either became one after making a pact with the Devil, or changed into one unwillingly as the result of a curse.

The person was said to change form during the hours of darkness. Some werewolves put on a wolf's skin to make the change, but most of them put a wolf-skin belt round their waists. Sometimes the person would have to remove his clothes and rub a secret ointment into his skin, while reciting the words of a spell. Others were simply transformed without the practice of any magic at all.

Once transformed, the werewolf was driven by a lust for blood and their only instinct was to kill and eat human victims, particularly if they were young.

If a werewolf was injured, the wound would remain on him after he had changed back to human form. There is a well-known werewolf legend told in Holland:

A young man once saw a huge wolf about to attack a girl who was sitting at the roadside. The young man fired an arrow into the wolf, which ran off howling. When the young man returned home he learned to his horror that the burgomaster, a respected man, was dying from a severe arrow wound in his side. On his deathbed the burgomaster confessed that he was the werewolf and begged for forgiveness.

In his human form the werewolf was said to have thick eyebrows which met in the middle across the bridge of his nose. He had pointed ears and he walked with a peculiar loping movement. It was believed in some places that a person turned inside-out when he changed into a werewolf and that his fur grew on the inside of his skin. For this reason, another sign of being a werewolf was for a person to have hairy palms.

Nowadays the majority of people see wolves only in the zoo or wild life parks and, thank goodness, the only time they will ever go in fear of werewolves is if they watch one on a late-night horror movie.

The beast of Gevaudan

On 19 June 1766 in a forest to the south of Auvergne in France, several hundred hunters armed with guns, pitchforks, and hatchets fearfully encircled a large section of woodland. As they moved cautiously forward the men wondered nervously whether they would be quick enough to kill their quarry, supposing it came into view, before it attacked and seriously injured some of them.

The hunt was on for a creature called the Wild Beast of Gevaudan, an enormous man-eating wolf which, for two years, had terrorized the countryside.

The monster wolf had killed and eaten more than a hundred men, women and children. The size and ferocity of it had amazed and terrified all who had seen it. Its teeth were long and razor-sharp. With one swing of its massive tail it could strike a lethal blow, and it was strong enough to carry off its victims in its formidable jaws.

The creature had fur of a reddish colour. Those who had come close to it said it gave off a smell that was beyond description. It seemed to have supernatural powers, for it could leap enormous heights and run at incredible speeds. It was utterly fearless. Not only had it attacked groups of people, but it had also set upon armed stagecoaches. Detachments of soldiers sent out to track down the wolf had been unsuccessful.

The people of Gevaudan were convinced that the beast was more than just a large and savage animal. They were sure that it was a *werewolf*—a man able to change his form to become a wolf at will. They were convinced that in human form it was a sorcerer of great evil, a man close to the Devil himself.

In the forest a group of the hunters froze to the spot. In the undergrowth ahead of them was the great wolf itself. The creature turned on them, its eyes red with fury and its mouth foaming. With demoniacal rage it sprang towards the men.

One of the hunters dropped to one knee, took careful aim, and fired. The wolf let out a howl, twisted in the air, and dropped to the ground. Its body jerked two or three times, then lay still. The scourge of the Beast of Gevaudan was over.

a party stunt

Here is a trick you can play on someone, as long as you are alone in a room with your victim. Explain that the room is haunted by a very shy, gentle ghost who sometimes appears, providing you are patient and relaxed.

Allow the victim to satisfy himself that there is no one hiding in the room. Then set two chairs in the middle of the room facing each other but fairly close together. Sit your victim in one, while you sit in the other.

Call the ghost very quietly with words such as, 'Are you there? Will you give us a sign?' Of course nothing happens. Explain to the victim that he is too tense. To help him relax, move both hands toward his eyes and rest your middle fingers, one on each eyelid. Tell him that the ghost will only appear in a very calm atmosphere and that it may make itself known by a current of air, a rapping, or even by actually touching him. But nothing is certain.

Again call the ghost, which will once more fail to appear. Take your hands away and reassure the victim that the ghost will do him no harm. Once again replace both hands on his eyes. Call the ghost again, but almost at once remove your hands. What you are doing here is establishing in your victim's mind that *both* your hands are being used to close his eyes.

Now go to replace your hands again, but this time, as soon as he closes his eyes, instead of using two hands to cover them, place two fingers of *one* hand on them. This leaves you with the other hand free.

Do not be in a hurry to use your free hand. Allow as much as twenty seconds to go by in perfect silence. Then quietly put your hand at the back of his head and very gently touch the hair on his neck. The more gently you do it, the better— don't forget you're supposed to be a ghost!

The effect can be quite hair-raising. After all, it is Hallowe'en!

You can have fun at your spooky party by inventing ways to make ghostly noises. You'll need a number of bottles, jugs, and buckets.

By getting your guests to blow gently across the tops of a number of different-sized bottles you can make an orchestra of weird moaning sounds.

Try whispering, humming, or breathing heavily into a bucket or large bin. This will produce quite a horrid, hollow, echoing sort of noise.

Ask the person who can make the most spine-chilling scream or demoniacal laugh to do it into a large jug or funnel, or through a paper tube.

Wet your finger and run it gently round and round the rim of a wine glass. With practice you will make a high-pitched sound that will at least set people's teeth on edge if it doesn't curdle their blood.

A really scary noise will come from this bull-roarer. To make it all you need is a ruler or thin piece of wood about 3 cm wide by 30 cm long (1½″ × 12″). Make a small hole in one end and attach a piece of string. When you revolve the piece of wood round and round your head it will make the most ghastly roaring noise.

The bull-roarer

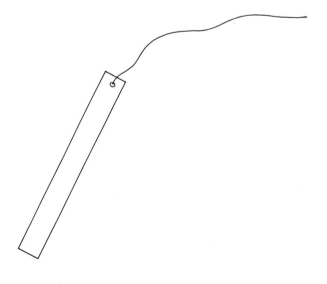

Forbidden sounds

When the banshees wail,
And the werewolves howl,
When the dead in the churchyard sigh.
When the witches scream,
And their demons hiss,
When you hear the song of the Lorelei.
When the bogies shout,
And when goblins yell.
When the shades call out
From the depths of Hell.
When the phantom drummer
Drums his drum,
When the midnight wraith
Whispers, 'Come, oh come . . .'
Then who will go?

Not I.

Eric James

Spooky jokes

What do you call a wicked old woman who lives by
the sea?
A sandwitch.

Why does a witch ride on a broom?
Vacuum cleaners have to be plugged into the wall.

What do witches go racing on?
Brrm ... brrm sticks.

What fruit does a vampire enjoy most?
Blood oranges.

Where do witches roost?
In Coven -tree.

Count of Horror

Of all the characters in horror stories one of the best known is Count Dracula, the gruesome bloodsucking count, living in his grim, foreboding castle in the mysterious country of Transylvania.

Count Dracula was invented by a writer named Bram Stoker.

Little did Stoker think, when he wrote his book *Dracula* in 1897, that almost a hundred years later the evil count would still capture the imagination of people who enjoy a frightening and spine-chilling horror story.

Although Bram Stoker had used his vivid imagination to dream up the character of Count Dracula, he based the country in which the story is set on a real place.

At the time when Stoker wrote the book, Transylvania was a remote part of Hungary. Set on an isolated plateau and surrounded on all sides by mountains, Transylvania was a secret, almost forgotten place.

The very name Transylvania means 'land beyond the forest'.

In his mind, Stoker conjured up a picture of grim-looking castles surrounded by dark, uninviting forests and woodlands.

He imagined superstitious peasants afraid to leave their homes at night. He saw them sitting round their fires after dark, telling each other blood-curdling stories full of horror and terrifying happenings.

It was when Bram Stoker was choosing Transylvania as a setting for his story that he came across the name Dracula. It was an ideal name for him to use for his main character.

Stoker found that just over five hundred years ago, part of Transylvania had a ruler called Prince Vlad.

Vlad had been an exceptionally cruel and terrifying figure. He called himself 'Vlad Dracula', since a 'dracul' meant a devil or dragon.

Vlad always carried the sign of the dragon on his shield. He was so feared and hated by his people that they called him 'Vlad the Impaler' because of his unpleasant habit of having anyone who opposed him impaled on a sharpened stake.

During Vlad's reign so many people were killed that it is no wonder that the name 'Dracula' became associated with cruelty and horror.

Using the legend of the vampire bat, borrowing the name Dracula, and setting the story in Transylvania, Stoker had all the ingredients for his horror story.

On an earlier occasion he had met a man whose teeth were like the fangs of a dog. Stoker remembered this, and Count Dracula came into being.

Vlad Dracula (or Vlad the Impaler).

88

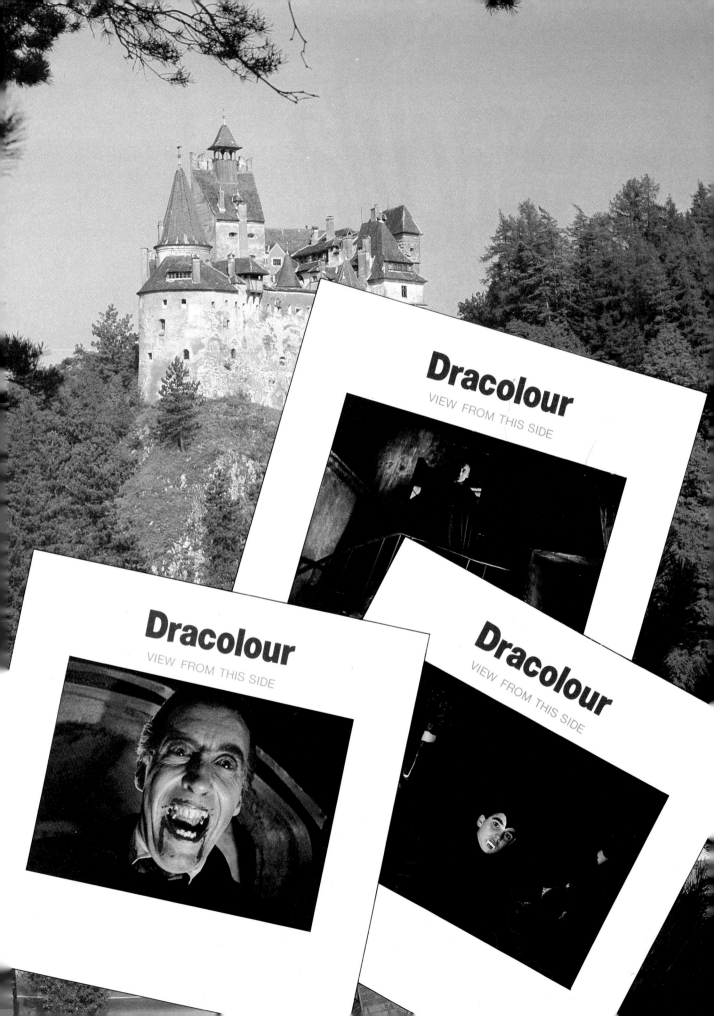

Dracolour

VIEW FROM THIS SIDE

Dracolour

VIEW FROM THIS SIDE

Dracolour

VIEW FROM THIS SIDE

AND A LEGEND IS BORN...

The hand of glory

This grisly-looking object is the hand of an executed criminal. It was cut from his body while he was still on the gallows.

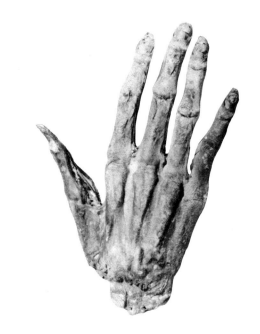

Up until the beginning of the nineteenth century, every superstitious burglar carried, as an essential part of his kit, a dead man's hand, just like this one.

The hand was thought to have magical properties which helped the burglar and protected him while he committed his crime.

It was supposed to open locks, make the thief invisible, and send the entire household into a drugged sleep, especially when the burglar chanted:

'Let those who rest more deeply sleep;
While those awake their vigils keep;
Oh, Hand of Glory shed thy light;
Direct us to our spoil tonight.'

If anyone did happen to see the burglar, or disturb him, the hand was supposed to send the person into a forgetful trance.

A Hand of Glory had to be carefully prepared. After it had been removed from the body it would be soaked in a solution of saltpetre, salt, and pepper, and then dried in the sun.

A candle was made from such strange ingredients as hanged man's fat, wax, and a substance called Lapland sesame. The candle was placed in the hand and lit while the robbery was taking place.

Here is the story of one robbery taken from the Irish Times of 13 January 1831 after a group of thieves had tried to break in to the house of Mr Napier of Longscrew in County Meath:

The men entered the house armed with a dead man's hand with a lighted candle in it, believing in the superstitious notion that a candle placed in a dead man's hand will not be seen and prevent those who may be asleep from waking. The inmates, however, were alarmed and the robbers fled leaving the hand behind them.

Thieves using a Hand of Glory to try to open a locked door.

92

a hand of glory

Here is an item for your spooky party that will really make your guests shudder.

It is a full-size hand with its fingers pointing up, but made out of jelly.

To make the hand, use a clean rubber glove. Make up a strong jelly, using less than the quantity of water recommended on the packet (say ¾).

Hang the rubber glove over the sink by holding it with strong Bulldog clips or clothes pegs and attaching these to a thin strip of wood. Fig. 1.

When the jelly liquid has cooled, pour it into the rubber glove and let it set firmly.

To remove the jelly from the glove, place it in the deep freeze, or freezer compartment of the fridge. Be careful not to have it pressing up against anything else. You could, at this stage, bend the fingers up a little more.

When the jelly is frozen, cut the glove off, using very fine scissors. Keep the jelly in the fridge until you are ready to serve it.

To make the hand look less bulky and less like the mould of a rubber glove, you can carve it into a better shape with a sharp knife. But only do this if the jelly is really firm.

You could be really ghoulish and make up some 'blood', using thick cornflour sauce coloured with cochineal, or red colouring, and pour this over the wrist and between the fingers.

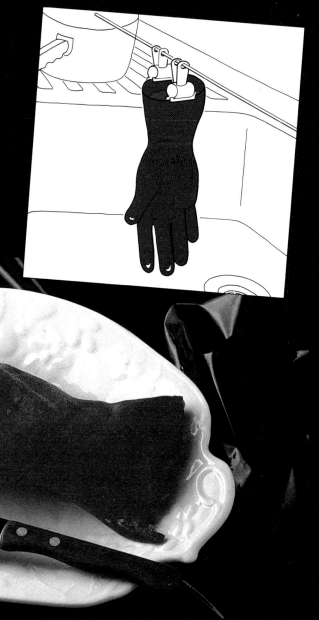

HOW TO MAKE
a skull cake

This skull cake could form the centrepiece for your party food. The cake itself is easy to make and delicious to eat.

You will need:

    1 lb (450 g) digestive biscuits
    8 oz (200 g) butter
    2 dessertspoons (approx 1 oz) cocoa
    2 tablespoons golden syrup
    2 tablespoons sugar
    This makes a flat shape approx 30 cm × 23 cm
       (12″ × 9″)
    Icing: 8 oz (200 g) icing (confectioners') sugar

Dissolve the butter, sugar, golden syrup, and cocoa in a saucepan until just warm.

Crush the digestive biscuits well in a mixing bowl using the end of a wooden rolling pin. Fig. 1. Add the liquid to this and mix well.

Now shape the mixture into the skull. Do this on to greaseproof paper on which you have drawn the outline of the skull. Make indentations for the eyes, nose, and mouth. Fig. 2.

Allow the cake to harden off in the fridge for a few hours.

To ice the cake:

Mix a little water with about 4 oz (100 g) of icing sugar (confectioners' sugar), keeping the mixture as stiff as possible.

Ice the skull, avoiding the eyes, nose, and mouth. When the icing has hardened, apply a second coat, using the remaining 100 g of sugar mixture.

Allow the cake to set completely in the fridge. Then remove it from the greaseproof paper and transfer it to a square cake board which has been covered with a black plastic bin-liner.

With the cake serve the eyeballs, frogs and mice (see p 32), and the jelly hand (see p 93).

You will have a lot of fun if you present the food at your party in a spooky way. Written fold-over labels will transform quite ordinary party food into something quite revolting. For example: Twiglet biscuits could be labelled 'Bats' Legs'; small gherkins could be called 'Pickled Slugs'; green jelly could bear the title 'Gangrene'; crisps could be 'Scales', and so on.

You'll have plenty of ideas of your own for this and you'll know how squeamish your guests are likely to be—you don't want to put them off completely!

To make a blue drink, add one or two drops of blue food colouring to a bottle of fizzy lemonade and stir in very slowly.

Fig. 1

Fig. 2

Graveyards

Would you like to spend an hour alone in a graveyard at the dead of night? Cemeteries and graveyards, especially old ones, can be very spooky places.

By tradition, however, each graveyard is said to be haunted by only one ghost—that is the Watcher who appears in the long white garment in which corpses were buried, called a shroud. This ghost was said to watch over the graveyard, guarding the dead and waiting for the moment to call on the next person in the parish who was due to die.

In the past, graveyards were especially terrifying when a phenomenon called *grave lights* occurred. This happened when the graves were dug in wet or marshy ground. Sometimes a gas was given off which, at night, produced an eerie glow.

It was customary for graves to be dug so that they ran from east to west. The body was then placed in it with the feet pointing towards the east. Then on Judgement Day the person would be able to rise facing the dawn. An old Welsh name for the east wind is 'the wind of dead men's feet'.

Few graves, if any, were dug from north to south. To do so was to show ill-will and a lack of respect to the people buried in them.

Graves were not usually dug in the ground to the north of a church unless the bodies were those of unbaptized babies or of people who had committed suicide. At one time, criminals were not buried in a grave-yard at all but at crossroads.

People used to consider it very unlucky for a loved one to be the first one buried in a new burial ground. It was believed that the dead person's soul would be stolen by the Devil. Very often the sexton would bury a dog in new ground, and this solved the problem.

Some epitaphs

A glassblower lies here at rest.
Who one day burst his noble chest
While trying, in a fit of malice,
To blow a second Crystal Palace.

Here lies the body of Edith Bone.
All her life she lived alone.
Until Death added the final S,
And put an end to her loneliness.

On a dentist

Stranger, approach this spot with gravity;
John Brown is filling his last cavity.

This is the grave of Mike O'Day,
Who died maintaining his right of way.
His right was clear, his will was strong,
But he's just as dead as if he'd been wrong.

Here lies I and my three daughters,
Killed by drinking the Cheltenham
   Waters.
If we had stuck to Epsom Salts,
We'd not been lying in these vaults.

Here lies my poor wife, much lamented.
She is happy and I am contented.

Here lies
Ezikial Aike
Aged 102
'The good
die young.'

On John So

So died John So.
So, so, did he so?
So did he live
And so did he die.
So, so did he so,
And so let him lie.

Oo-oo-ah-ah

Get ready, when you sing this song to let out a terrifying and blood-curdling shriek at the very end.

A woman in the churchyard sat,
  Oo-oo, oo-oo, ah-ah, ah-ah!
She was very short and fat,
  Oo-oo, oo-oo, ah-ah, ah-ah!
She saw three corpses carried in,
  Oo-oo, oo-oo, ah-ah, ah-ah!
Very tall and very thin,
  Oo-oo, oo-oo, ah-ah, ah-ah!

Woman to the corpses said,
  Oo-oo, oo-oo, ah-ah, ah-ah!
Shall I be like you when I'm dead?
  Oo-oo, oo-oo, ah-ah, ah-ah!
Corpses to the woman said,
  Oo-oo, oo-oo, ah-ah, ah-ah!
Yes, you'll be like us when you're dead,
  Oo-oo, oo-oo, ah-ah, ah-ah!

Woman to the corpses said,
  WAAAAAGGGGGHHHHH!

GHOSTS

Ghosts

A cold and starry darkness moans
　　And settles wide and still
Over a jumble of tumbled stones
　　Dark on a darker hill.

An owl among those shadowy walls,
　　Gray against gray
Of ruins and brittle weeds, calls
　　And a soundless swoops away.

Rustling over scattered stones
　　Dancers hover and sway,
Drifting among their own bones
　　Like the webs of the Milky Way.

Harry Behn

The tavern of the dead

The audience take their seats in a gloomy hall hung with black. Around the room are coffins in the place of tables. On each one a candle is burning. The hall is called *Le Cabaret du Néant*, or The Tavern of the Dead.

One of the audience is invited to seat himself at a table which stands on a darkened stage at one end of the hall. Suddenly, a ghostly figure appears beside the man and sets a bottle and glass on the table. The man sees nothing, and is asked to motion with his arm. In doing so, his arm passes clean through the spectre's body.

About a hundred years ago illusions such as this were a popular form of entertainment in many of the big cities of Europe and the USA. Ghosts and mysterious figures were produced by having a piece of glass across part of the stage. The ghostly figures were created by having actors hidden from the audience but reflected in the glass by use of special lighting.

Pepper's ghost

The audience is hushed and expectant. It is the final act of the play. On the stage, quite alone, is the villain of the piece. In the scenes before, this man showed himself to be one of extreme cruelty who would commit murder to achieve his wicked ends.

Suddenly, a look of terror passes over the villain's face and a nervous tremor runs over the audience.

The ghostly figure of a woman who was killed by the villain in an earlier scene now glides across the stage. The woman is clearly a ghost. Her form is transparent and insubstantial. Furniture and the wall behind can be seen through her ghostly shape.

The 'ghost' raises an accusing arm and the villain, overcome with fear and remorse, falls to his knees to beg for mercy.

The appearance of ghosts was a popular theatre illusion in days gone by. The illustration shows how the effect was achieved.

A large sheet of glass was fixed at an angle in front of the stage between the actors and the audience. The angle was such that when a strong light was played on someone out of view to the audience, a reflection of the person would appear on the glass giving the impression that the figure was present on the stage.

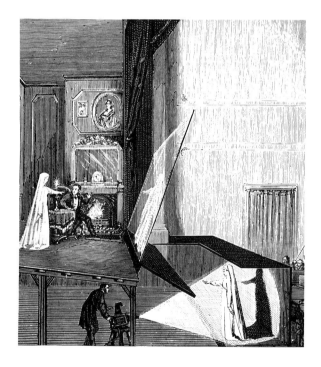

The effect of a ghost appearing on the stage was named Pepper's Ghost after the inventor of the illusion.

HOW TO MAKE

your own ghost

You will need:

- A large empty cornflake carton 22 × 32 cm (8¾" × 12½")
- A piece of glass or perspex 26 × 7 cm (10¾" × 2¾")
- latex glue, sticky tape,
- card, felt tip pens,
- scissors, matt black paint.

Cut the front off the carton and cut out a section as shown.

Use the sides of the removed section to rebuild the walls of the box as shown in Fig. 1.

On white card draw a ghost approx 4 cm (1½") high, and draw an arch approx 5.5 cm (2¾") high. The figure will need to be able to stand in the arch. Fig. 2.

Cut holes approx 4 cm × 2.5 cm (1½" × 1") as shown in Fig. 3.

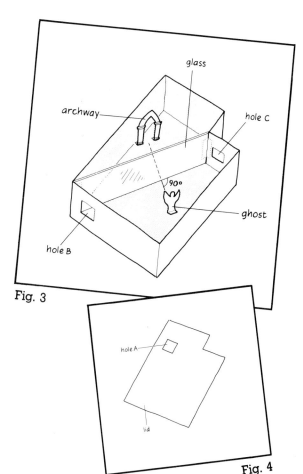

Fig. 3

Fig. 4

Fig. 1

Fig. 2

Paint the inside of the box black. When dry fit the piece of glass using sticky tape, making sure it is not tilted. Fig. 3.

Glue the ghost and the arch in position as shown, making sure that the ghost is the same distance from the glass as the arch is behind, and that both are at right angles to it. Fig. 3.

Make the lid as shown, cutting a 2.5 cm (1") square hole so that it will be positioned over the arch. Fig. 4. Fit the lid on and tape it down so that no light enters at any edge.

Use the light from a flashlight or anglepoise lamp to view the ghost. First look through hole B and hold the box so that light enters through hole A in the lid. You should see the archway by itself.

Cover hole A and angle the light so that it enters through hole C. The ghost should then appear in the archway.

101

A ghost on film

This photograph of the altar of Newby Church in Yorkshire should have been quite ordinary. It was a perfectly ordinary day when it was taken. The vicar had arranged for a series of photographs to be taken of his church. He planned to have them printed as postcards which he could then sell to raise money for the church fund.

The photographer had chosen a sunny day to take the pictures. He had spent time in getting the best views both inside and outside the church. The last few pictures were to be taken of the nineteenth century altar, which is the centre-piece of the church. It has an attractive stained glass window behind it. The vicar hoped it would make one of his best picture postcards.

The camera was set up on its stand and the pictures were taken. Nothing unusual was seen. Perhaps there was a sudden slight chill in the air—a cool draught, perhaps, which blew past and was gone, such as might be felt sometimes in large buildings—but nothing else. The photographer was well pleased with his morning's work.

When the prints were ready and the photographer looked through them, he noticed on one the figure of a monk standing on the altar steps. How could the monk have appeared on the photograph? Could this really be a ghost? If so, how could it have been seen by the camera, yet by no one else at the time the picture was taken.

The prints were shown to the vicar, but he too was baffled. He did not think his church was haunted. No one had ever seen the ghostly monk before. What could be the answer to the mystery?

Experts examined the camera and the film. They agreed that this was a genuine photograph. The film had not been touched and the camera wasn't able to take double exposures (this is when two pictures are taken on the same piece of film by mistake).

The answer to the mystery is simple. The photograph was taken by opening the shutter of the camera for a few seconds. This meant that the picture was taken very slowly. So slowly, in fact, that if someone walked across in front of the camera quickly enough, it would not be able to take his photograph, unless he stood still for a moment. And if he happened to be wearing a hooded robe, and had a white sheet over his face....

The amazing Mr Home

During the second half of the nineteenth century people became fascinated by a phenomenon known as spiritualism. This is the practice of trying to make contact with the dead. Usually this is done through a medium—a person who claims to have special powers which allow the spirits of dead people to talk through him.

It all started with the Fox sisters in Hydesville, New York State, in 1848. Two young girls, Kate and Margarette Fox, caused a sensation by claiming to make contact with the spirit of a man they said had been killed in the house where they were living.

The Fox sisters started a craze which swept through the country and spread to Europe. Soon millions of people were attending meetings called *seances* where they witnessed such things as mysterious rappings on tables, disembodied voices, automatic writing, and luminous apparitions. At some seances heavy objects floated through the air or musical instruments played by themselves.

Unfortunately many mediums were frauds, and people who came to a seance hoping to hear a genuine message from their dead relatives were cheated, often by crude conjuring tricks.

One medium who baffled researchers

Daniel Dunglas Home.

A group of people holding a seance.

103

and scientists was a man called Daniel Dunglas Home. Home was known as a physical *medium*. This is someone who claims that through him the spirit world is able to manipulate things and move objects about.

Home's powers were extraordinary. He was able to make small items vanish and reappear in a different part of the room. He could make objects, some as heavy as a piano, levitate (rise up in the air) all by themselves. In his presence musical instruments would play, as if by invisible hands. Sometimes he himself would levitate, or he would levitate other people.

Throughout his career as a medium

Home was never caught in the act of fraud or trickery. He held many seances in bright light and he did not receive payment for them. He was always willing for people to investigate what he did, and he was happy to demonstrate his powers to the most disbelieving of them.

At a seance at the court of Napoleon III in France on 12 January 1863, Home caused a tablecloth to levitate from the table, even though he was some distance away and the room was fully lit. While the table was being examined to see if Home had used trick apparatus, it gave off a series of raps that seemed to come from the wood of the table itself.

One man who investigated Home's amazing ability was a famous scientist called Sir William Crookes. Once Crookes enclosed an accordion in a metal cage so that Home could not reach it. Despite this, during the seance, the accordion rose up in the cage and played a tune.

Another strange phenomenon which Home was able to achieve was that of stretching his body. He would increase his body length by as much as six inches, even though as many as six witnesses were holding on to him.

Home's favourite trick was to levitate himself. It was claimed that people hung on to his legs while he rose up in the air, and Sir William Crookes himself witnessed Home levitate a chair with a woman sitting in it.

Perhaps most amazing of all was Home's apparent ability to handle red-hot coal without burning himself. It seems that he could take a piece of glowing coal from the fire, hold it in both hands, and blow on it until it was almost white hot.

No one has ever been able to explain how Home was able to achieve his astonishing feats. It is unlikely that he used apparatus and he did not have accomplices to help him. Many of his seances were held in other people's homes, so it would have been difficult for him to fake his amazing effects.

How did he do it? The truth is that nobody knows.

Daniel Home levitates himself in front of a group of astonished onlookers.

HOW TO
levitate someone

This is a lighthearted stunt to try at your party.

Get someone heavy to sit on a chair and ask four people to try and lift him, using the flat part of their hands which should be placed under the person's upper arms and thighs. The lifters will succeed in raising the person a little way.

Now get each lifter in turn to place a hand, palm down, on the person's head so that all hands are eventually placed on top of each other. The lifters should then press gently *not* firmly.

All five people now take a deep breath and hold it while they count to twenty. When this is done everyone must breathe out, and the lift should immediately be attempted.

This time the person will be raised considerably more than the first time.

The Author is levitated at the Hallowe'en party.

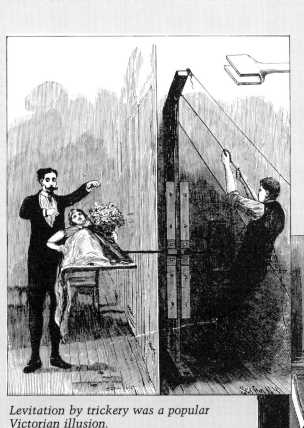

Levitation by trickery was a popular Victorian illusion.

And so to bed

Think what it must have been like in the days when there were no electric lights and when people had only a spluttering candle or glimmering taper to light their way to bed.

Imagine them climbing the dark stairs and seeing only as far ahead as the dim light of the candle would reach. Imagine the wavering shadows as the candle-flame flickered in the draughty bedroom, while outside, in a night as dark as pitch, the wind moaned about the house and sighed through the cracks and crevices in the walls and floors.

People were very careful, especially on All Hallows' Eve, to protect themselves from harmful witches and evil spirits. Doorways would be hung with garlic, laurel or bay leaves, and horseshoes.

Before going to bed the fire was put out to prevent a hobgoblin being attracted inside to warm himself. Fire-irons were placed on the empty grate in the sign of the cross. This was done to keep a witch from entering the house by way of the chimney.

Brooms were carefully put away in cupboards, in case a witch should spirit one out of the house to ride on it and bring bad luck to the household.

Lastly all doors and windows were securely locked and the keys removed. As an added safeguard, the sign of the cross was made over the keyholes to stop some witch or warlock from slipping through them.

Of course there were still dangers, even in sleep. To keep a baby safe from a witch, a knife would be placed at the bottom of the cot. Some parents would slip a piece of bread, blessed by a priest, under a child's pillow. They would say words similar to these as they did so:

Bring the holy crust of bread.
Lay it underneath the head.
'Tis a certain charm to keep
Hags away while children sleep.

Before they went to sleep people would speak the words of a charm. The charm had to be repeated aloud before the eyes closed. This one is still said by people, even to this day:

Matthew, Mark, Luke and John,
Bless the bed that I lie on.
If I die before I wake,
I pray the Lord my soul to take.
Four corners to my bed,
Four angels round my head,
One to watch and one to pray,
Two to keep the Devil away.

For when we dream...

The human mind works at two levels. When we are awake, our thoughts, our actions, and our responses are all controlled by the conscious level of the mind. The conscious mind constantly responds, through our five senses, to what is happening in the world around us and we are aware of the dimensions of time, space, and distance. Throughout the day, in a state of wakeful consciousness, we focus our attention, direct our thoughts, exercise our will, and make judgements and decisions.

During sleep, the subconscious level of the mind comes into operation. The subconscious mind could be said to work 'beneath the surface'. In a way it is a sort of opposite, or counterpart, to the conscious mind. In it are stored our memories of past experiences, many of which we can no longer recall in our conscious mind. These memories include emotions such as fear,

guilt, likes, and dislikes; and these may make us behave in a way we do not fully understand—for example, we may be afraid of dogs for reasons which are locked deep within our subsconscious mind.

Sometimes during the day, our attention may wander. In this state we day-dream, and thoughts or images enter our minds without our really knowing why. This is because the subconscious mind has come to the surface and has triggered off our thoughts. When this happens we may be in an almost trance-like state, only half aware of our real surroundings.

When our subconscious mind takes over, it is not limited by the restraints of reality. Dreams are often fantastic and improbable. What happens in them is not governed by any physical laws. We might, for example, dream that we are flying, or dream that we are on the moon.

Through dreams, our subconscious mind acts out our hopes and fears and plays

out experiences which release for us emotions we can not, or do not, show in real life. Dreams, then, are an important part of our emotional make-up.

Research has shown that dreaming is as necessary as eating or drinking. In some experiments, some years ago, volunteers were woken up whenever their brain waves, which were being recorded, showed that they had begun to dream. After only a few nights without dreams the volunteers became irritable and anxious, and had difficulty in concentrating. A second group of volunteers were woken up several times during the night, but not when they were dreaming. Despite their interrupted nights this group of volunteers had none of the troubles of the first group.

All of us dream at night, not once but four or five times. Dreams occur in a regular pattern so that, during an eight-hour period of sleep, we dream about every ninety minutes. And the length of each dream gets longer as the night goes on.

Scientists have recorded the depth of sleep by measuring brain waves. They have found that first we sink into a deep sleep. Then our levels of sleep rise and fall. As we dream our eyes flicker rapidly under our eyelids as if we are following the dream with our eyes. Some people claim that they hardly ever dream, but this is not true. And if you think you didn't dream last night, it is because you have forgotten what you dreamt.

Dreams can sometimes be very vivid, and some can be very frightening or disturbing. Everyone has nightmares from time to time and these may occur because a person is unwell or suffering from shock or stress. Nightmares are quite common in young children who have been scared by a story or a television programme.

Can dreams come true? People have certainly experienced vivid dreams about things which later actually happened. Charles Dickens, the famous author, told how he once dreamed about a young woman. When he woke up he could see her clearly in his mind's eye. Later that day he met the young woman. He had never seen her before, and yet she looked and dressed exactly as he had seen her in his dream.

Many people find that when they have a problem to solve, or when they are unable to work something out, the answer will come to them in a dream. The subconscious mind has continued to search for a solution while the conscious mind is asleep. For example, Mozart, the composer, spoke of finished musical pieces that came to him in his dreams. Many authors, composers, and even scientists rely on these creative dreams to help them in their work.

When a dream came true

In the early hours of the morning of 2 May 1812, Mr John Williams, a respected mine owner of Redruth in Cornwall, woke up from a disturbing dream. The dream was so vivid that Mr Williams woke his wife and described it to her. She said that he had eaten too well the evening before and told him to go back to sleep.

Twice more during the night Mr Williams had the dream.

He dreamed that he was in the lobby of the House of Commons — a place well known to him. A small man, dressed in a blue coat and white waistcoat, entered the lobby. Immediately another man stepped up to the small man, drew out a pistol, and fired it at point-blank range at him. The shot struck the victim under the left breast. A patch of blood appeared on the man's waistcoat as he fell to the floor.

In his dream, Mr Williams was told that the man was the Chancellor of the Exchequer.

The following day, Mr Williams was so troubled by his dream that he considered going all the way to London to warn someone in the Government. His friends and family persuaded him not to, saying that he would become a laughing stock and that nobody would take him seriously.

If Mr Williams had made his dream known in London, a small part of history might have been different. A little over a week afterwards, Mr Spencer Perceval, Prime Minster and Chancellor of the Exchequer, was murdered in the House of Commons just as Williams had seen in his extraordinary dream.

The assassin was a man called

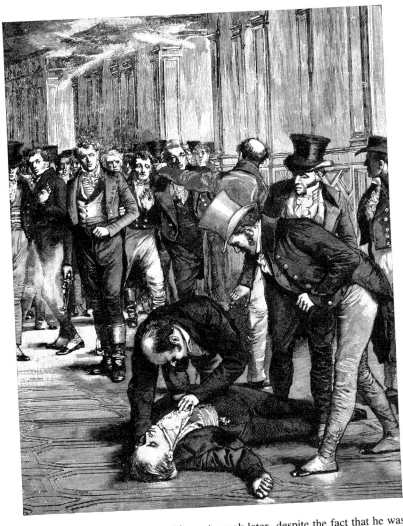

Bellingham, who nursed a bitter grievance against the Government and in particular, against Perceval.

It seems clear that Bellingham was insane, for on 11 May, he waited quite openly in the lobby of the House and, when Perceval arrived, he fired. the Prime Minister died almost immediately and Bellingham made no attempt to escape.

In the confusion that followed, an offer of the House shouted out, 'Where is the rascal who fired?' Bellingham calmly stepped forward and said, 'I am the unfortunate man.'

Bellingham was tried and executed a

week later, despite the fact that he was obviously not responsible for his actions.

Meanwhile, in Cornwall, Mr Williams anxiously read the newspapers for several days after his dream, and began to believe that his dream was, as his wife had said, due to nothing more than over-eating.

Then, on 13 May ,his second son returned from Truro. He came into the room where his father was sitting and blurted out the news: 'Father, your dream has come true. Mr Perceval has been shot in the lobby of the House of Commons.'

THE GHOST DOSSIER

Do you believe in ghosts?

If you asked people what would make them believe that ghosts exist, they'd probably tell you that they would only be absolutely certain if they had seen one for themselves. After all, seeing is believing.

How about you? Do you believe in ghosts? Supposing, for example, you were to find yourself in the grounds of an old ruined house or castle. If a misty figure, wearing the clothes of long ago, were to appear; and if the figure were to glide along, passing through walls or solid objects, then you could be fairly certain that what you were seeing was a ghost.

Perhaps you don't need to be convinced. You may be the kind of person who feels sure that there are such things as ghosts, even though the nearest you have come to seeing one is by watching a spooky programme on television.

You may be willing to believe in ghosts simply because you have heard stories about them or because so many ordinary people claim to have seen one. And if someone you know and respect, one of your relations or a close friend, has experienced seeing one, you may be even more convinced.

What is a ghost?

What is a ghost? Well, there are almost as many answers to that question as there are different sorts of ghost, from transparent, headless phantoms in Elizabethan costume who haunt old houses, to strange photographic-looking faces which appear mysteriously on walls and ceilings.

There are ghosts in houses, hotels, hospitals, theatres, ships, and even in aeroplanes. They appear in castles and churches, on old battlefields, at crossroads, in graveyards, at sea, and in forests. There are ghosts of revengeful monks, weeping nuns, shrouded corpses, chained prisoners, drummer boys, ladies in white, coachmen and horses, battalions of soldiers, and racing-drivers in racing-cars.

Although it is often thought that they show themselves only after the hours of darkness, most ghosts are seen in full daylight.

They may whisper, sigh, groan, sob, sing, shriek, or scream. Some are invisible, others seem to be quite real and solid, only showing themselves to be ghosts when they disappear before the eyes of the astonished onlookers. Some ghosts are gentle and serene, bringing about a feeling of calm and peace; others are anguished and tormented, apparently doomed to endure centuries of suffering and remorse. There are pathetic ghosts who place a clammy hand on the victim's skin, and there are other more exuberant manifestations who inflict a bruising grip on an arm or leg, or even cause the victim to be thrown out of bed.

Very occasionally people have encountered spirits who give out such a feeling of evil and malevolence that the unlucky onlooker has been filled with indescribable terror and dread.

The folk-lore tradition

Different parts of the world have different types of ghost, many of which belong to the *folk-lore tradition*. This means that popular stories about ghosts and hauntings are told and retold so many times that people link them with certain places even though few people, if any, could claim to have seen ghosts there.

You may live near an old house or building which is reputed to have a ghost that walks in its grounds or corridors. Probably the only real thing about traditional ghosts are the stories that people tell about them!

On the other hand, thousands of ordinary people claim to have witnessed a ghostly manifestation of one kind or another. Many people believe they have seen a ghost on one occasion, other people have had an astonishing number and variety of experiences.

If you meet a ghost ...

So what is a ghost, and what should you do if you see one? The first thing to say is that you will almost certainly have no need to be frightened. Your ghost may appear to be so much like the figure of an ordinary person that, at first, you may not even realize it is a ghost.

The moment you become aware of one, stay still and observe it closely. No ghost has ever been known to harm anyone, so it is absurd to imagine that a ghost would single you out especially to give you a scare. It is more likely that your ghost will not even be conscious of you, and if you move suddenly, or make a noise, it may disappear.

There are various theories to explain ghosts. Here are just a few of them.

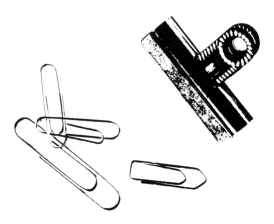

The Energy Trace Theory

The figure on the bed

A fascinating theory about one sort of ghost is given by a Canadian writer called Victoria Brandon. As a child, Victoria lived in an old, rambling farmhouse. When she was eight years old, some sort of family reunion took place. So many relatives came to stay at the house that there were hardly enough places for them all to sleep.

The children—and there were nine of them—were packed into an attic bedroom. The room was never used in the ordinary way since it was bare and uncomfortable. It was cold in the winter, hot in the summer, and it had a ceiling that sloped almost to the floor. It also had an old bedstead which had been there for years and was too big and cumbersome to be moved.

It was just the sort of room that would have been used by a servant girl in the days when the farmhouse was part of a farm.

The nine children, excited by each other's company and keyed up from being in strange surroundings, took a long time to settle down to sleep.

During the night, Victoria woke up to see a figure sitting on her bed. In her sleepy state, and in the semi-darkness, she thought at first that it must be one of her cousins, but gradually she realized that it was someone she had never seen before.

The figure was that of a thin-looking woman with greying hair pulled back into a tight knot at the back of her head. The woman wore a grey dress made of a coarse, cheap, cottony material. She sat with her head bowed and her shoulders hunched as if she was overcome with absolute misery and despair.

The woman seemed completely unware of the sleeping children and appeared to take no notice of Victoria. She looked neither frightening nor dangerous. Her appearance, if anything, was pitiful rather than sinister or threatening. However, realizing that she was seeing a ghost, Victoria pulled the covers over her head and didn't look out again until the morning.

When she told her parents what she had seen, they told her she must have been dreaming. But was she? Even though no one had ever seen the ghost before and no one has seen it since, Victoria is convinced that she was wide awake when she saw the apparition of the woman in grey.

So what did she see that night? Why did the image of someone who presumably once occupied that particular room appear before Victoria's eyes?

It is hard to believe that the actual spirit of a lonely and unfortunate woman should, willingly or unwillingly, return to the dismal bedroom. The room had no history of tragedy or violence in connection with any servant girl who lived there in the past.

If the room was haunted it would mean that the ghostly presence of the woman frequently sat there, fully aware of her surroundings and still enduring the miseries and hardships she had suffered during life. This seems very hard to accept if we believe that the souls of the departed pass to a better world.

The energy trace theory

Human beings, like all living things, produce a sort of energy. This energy is rather like an electric charge. It is given off particularly strongly during moments of extreme emotion, such as anger, fear, hatred, grief, and so on.

The energy cannot be seen in the normal way, but it somehow remains—or leaves a trace in the atmosphere—for a brief time after a person has gone.

It may be that some people give off more energy than others, but it seems reasonable to suppose that people don't give off strong energy forces during the course of their daily lives—in going to work, for example, or when shopping at the supermarket.

However, if a crisis occurs and a person has to face sudden violence or extreme danger; or if someone is in a state of intense emotion for a long time, and is suffering, perhaps, from jealousy, guilt, or unhappiness, then a powerful field of energy is released and impressed on the physical surroundings.

Now, supposing that much later, perhaps even after several years, there is a disturbance in that place (such as the case when the nine highly excited children were put to bed in that out-of-the-way bedroom). When that happens, the energy trace is formed into an image which becomes visible for a short time.

This might be compared to the way that a film is developed. The image, recorded by the camera, shows up only when the film is processed and treated with a special chemical solution. In the same way an energy trace appears in the air only under certain conditions.

It could be that the unhappy woman in grey, seen by Victoria Brandon, was just such an image. The effect that the children's excitment had on the normally undisturbed room may have created the conditions for an energy trace of the woman to develop and show up on the highly-charged atmosphere.

Many people believe that the theory of the energy trace is convincing. They argue that it explains why some ghosts appear, then fade away, and why they seem not to notice any human onlookers and never try to communicate with them.

It would account, too, for why ghosts appear to step through walls or closed doors or walk on levels that are no longer there.

It is also thought that particular places or certain physical conditions produce more energy traces than others. For example, far more apparitions are seen in moist climates than in dry ones. Ghosts are frequently seen before a thunderstorm, when there is considerable electrical activity in the air.

The presence of certain people—those we call psychic—may produce forces which can cause an energy trace to materialize. People who have seen a ghost are likely to have done so on more than one occasion.

There are, however, arguments against the energy trace theory. In some places—battlefields, scenes of disaster, hospitals, churches, and so on, the discharge of human energy must have been enormous, yet in many of these places ghostly images are never seen.

Levels of

Consciousness

The case of the ghostly dog.

The Irish author, Diarmuid MacManus, tells how, when he was a boy his teenage sister gave a puppy to their older cousins in Dublin. The dog was a lovable Scots terrier called Bogey.

Bogey became a lively and affectionate member of the family, and Diarmuid and his sister looked forward to seeing the little dog scurrying up to greet them when they called at their cousins' house.

Alas, the span of a dog's life is short compared to that of a human, and after twelve years Bogey died and was, for a time, sadly missed by everyone.

The years rolled by, and almost forty years later the only cousin left was Alice who was then an elderly woman. Diarmuid's sister retired from a busy life and went to live in the west of Ireland. But she called on Alice whenever she came to Dublin.

It was on such a visit that a strange thing happened. Diarmuid's sister drove round to the house to see the old lady and, going up to the front door, she both knocked and rang. On each side of the door was a tall narrow window which not only helped to light the hall but also allowed anyone outside to look in. Diarmuid describes what happens next:

'As her cousin was a long time in coming, my sister peered through the right-hand window before deciding whether it was time to ring again. However, as she hesitated, the dining-room door opened and Alice appeared to answer the bell.

But she had hardly stepped into the hall when a little Scots terrier also appeared from the darkness of the back of the hall and came racing along, looking up at Alice as he passed her and running on till he disappeared from my sister's sight near the foot of the door.'

"So Alice has been given another dog," thought my sister. "How nice! But she can't possibly look after it. No it can't be that. Perhaps there is a visitor here who has brought it."

Soon the door was opened but no dog was to be seen. My sister opened her mouth to ask about it, but fortunately stopped in time as something in her subconscious mind cried out in warning, "It's Bogey. It's Bogey!' Then it came to her forcibly that it was so, of course it was.

'She had undoubtably seen the same old collar with the same medal with his address on it - and the very same dog, too. There he had been, first looking up at his mistress in the same fond way and then coming on to welcome the visitor just as he had done in days gone by - so very far gone by!'

Diarmuid's sister saw Bogey so clearly that at first she thought that she was seeing a real flesh-and-blood dog. She insists that the phantom dog was aware that the bell had been rung; that he looked up at his mistress as he approached her and swerved a little so as to avoid her before running out of sight as he reached the door.

Diarmuid asks 'Had Bogey always been there, keeping watch over his old mistress and was it that my sister merely happened to be mentally tuned into him at the moment?'

Levels of consciousness

Imagine being somewhere where you need to be really alert and fully on your toes. Maybe it's the first day back at school, or perhaps you are making a journey to a strange place all by yourself.

In such situations you would be wide awake and completely aware of your surroundings. All your five senses—sight, sound, smell, taste and touch, would be aroused and you would be fully conscious of everything that is going on around you.

Now imagine a different situation. You are awake, but completely relaxed. Maybe you are reading or listening to music. Perhaps you are at school in a stuffy classroom nearing the end of a long and boring lesson.

You are so relaxed that your mind wanders and, even though you aren't asleep, you lose touch with your surroundings. A series of pictures comes into your mind's eye. You begin to daydream and you see yourself as the hero of some exciting adventure or other.

You can see from this that the mind operates at different levels of consciousness between deep sleep and alert wakefulness. Scientists are able to measure brain activity on sensitive recording equipment called an EEG (electroencephalograph).

EEG readings show that the brain gives off rhythms which alter according to different kinds of brain activity. Brain waves recorded while a sleeping person is dreaming are different from those recorded while he is wide awake doing a mathematics test.

Scientists call the various patterns of rhythms *states*.

Beta state, for example, is a person's normal, busy, slightly anxious waking state. *Delta* and *theta* states are those associated with sleep.

When a person is awake but feels no need to concentrate, the mind may become relaxed and disengaged and the brain rhythms may change to an *alpha* state. During these moments unrelated images and memories pop into the mind without the person being aware of the reason.

Everyone has experienced brief moments, sometimes just a few seconds, when the mind wanders, or slips into an *alpha* state. People often fail to hear something that was said to them. 'I'm sorry, I was miles away,' they say apologetically. And sometimes a person's mind can wander without them even realizing or noticing it.

When Diarmuid MacManus's sister saw an image of Bogey joyfully racing to answer the door, did she really see a phantom or did an image of the dog well up from her subconscious memory and flash across her mind's eye?

Many visions, like that of Bogey, are triggered off by people's hopes and fears or their likes and dislikes, or stem from memories and past experiences, all of which are stored in the subconscious mind.

It is possible that many 'ghosts' are really visions that arise out of a state of mind. Diarmuid's sister, remembering happier days long ago, recalled Bogey when her mind was relaxed and that memory was projected by her subconscious almost like a film.

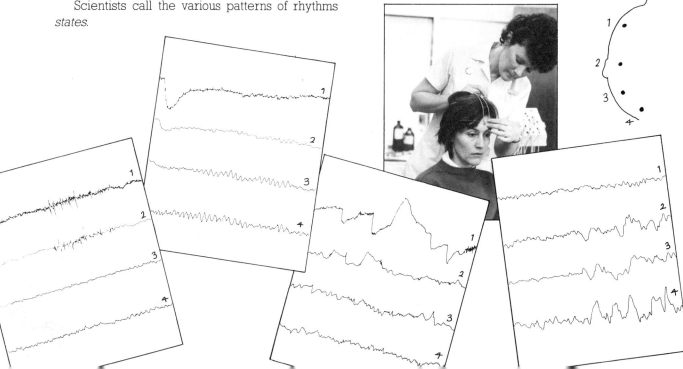

The Poltergeist File

The Case of Annemarie

During 1967 and 1968 extraordinary things began to happen at the offices of a well-known and respectable law firm in the small West German town of Rosenheim.

It all began when the telephone started to ring frequently and for no apparent reason. The Post Office was asked to investigate but could find no reason for the telephone's strange behaviour.

Then other electrical equipment began to play up. Light bulbs exploded and automatic fuses blew. Neon lights high up in the ceiling kept on going out and were later found to have worked themselves loose from their sockets. Developing fluid mysteriously seeped out of the photocopying machine, and sharp bangs and reports were heard all over the building.

Strangest of all were the hundreds and hundreds of telephone calls to the speaking clock, which had been automatically registered without the calls ever having been made.

Electrical experts were asked to research the problem and were amazed when huge surges of electrical power were recorded on their monitoring equipment. Where was the extra power coming from? The experts disconnected the normal power supply and were even more mystified to find that certain electrical items went on working by themselves.

Finally the question was asked, 'Could the strange events have something to do with poltergeists?' A second team of experts was sent for who specialized in a phenomenon known as PK, *psychokinesis*. (PK is a force which comes from a human source and has the power to influence objects. For example, it can make things move, or even fly through the air. In many instances of PK, lights have been known to switch themselves on and off.).

It was noticed that the extraordinary events occurred whenever a nineteen year-old girl, whose name was Annemarie, was working in the building. The investigators observed her closely, and found that when Annemarie walked along the corridor, lights hanging from the ceiling would start to swing with increasing force and carry on doing so for some time after she had gone by.

When it became clear that the girl was the source of the poltergeist activity, things go worse. Paintings began to spin round on the walls, drawers kept flying open, and a huge set of shelves moved all by themselves.

With the increased activity, the girl became more and more upset and finally grew hysterical. At last it was decided to dismiss her and find her another job in a different law office.

As soon as she was removed from the place where the trouble occurred, no further activity took place. The girl, who was unhappy at the first office, settled down without any more of the unnerving events happening again. Shortly after, she became engaged to be married and her life continued quite normally.

What, Poltergeist?

Until recently it was believed that poltergeists were troublesome ghosts who picked on households and, for a time, made life very unpleasant for everyone who lived there. *Poltergeist* is a German word and means *noisy spirit*.

There is almost no end to the kinds of tricks which poltergeists play. Their favourite activity, apart from making a noise, is to cause objects to fly through the air. They seem especially fond of making plates and dishes float about as if being carried by invisible hands.

They also like to open doors and windows, switch on lights, turn taps on, empty out the contents of drawers and cupboards, move items of furniture about, strip the bedclothes from beds, and rearrange the objects in a room.

Their more dangerous and unpleasant activities have included starting small fires, pouring quantities of water on floors and carpets, tipping people out of bed, pinching people or pulling hair, and making small objects whizz about, narrowly missing people's heads.

Among their most amazing accomplishments is the ability to make solid objects vanish into nothing and then make them materialize in a completely different place.

In recent years, investigators have become convinced that poltergeists are not ghosts at all, so the term *noisy spirit* is misleading. Research has shown, in almost every case, that poltergeist activity has centered round a person—usually someone quite young.

The evidence suggests that the person concerned is unknowingly responsible for what happens and that the disturbances are due to a sort of energy which is somehow released without that person realizing it.

The name given to this energy, or force, is psychokinesis (PK). *Psyche* is a Greek word meaning *soul* or mind; *kinesis* means *motion* or *movement*—hence, *movement by the mind*.

Because in cases of so-called poltergeist activity a person has no control of what happens or how often the disturbances occur, researchers prefer to call it RSPK. This stands for recurrent spontaneous psychokinesis. The word *recurrent* means *keeps on happening*, and *spontaneous* means it happens *by itself, outside anyone's control*.

It is generally agreed that RSPK occurs when an individual is extremely unhappy or disturbed and yet does not have a way to give vent to pent-up feelings.

A simple way to think of this is to imagine someone wanting to fly into a violent temper but not being able to do so and having to bottle up all the rage and anger inside.

In a case of RSPK, however, a person is not usually aware of having such strong feelings because they are so deep-seated. In one case, for example, a boy of ten had had to live in a hotel with a very strict aunt after his parents had died. When RSPK began to affect the hotel, the cause was traced to the boy. Sensibly the aunt allowed him to live in a children's home, and the trouble ceased at once.

pō′lō n. Game of Eastern origin like hockey played on horseback with long-handled mallet (~-**stick**); ~-**neck,** high round turned-over collar; WATER[1] *polo.* [Balti, = ball]
pō′lōcrŏsse n. Game played on horseback with long-handled stick having net at end. [f. prec. + LACROSSE]
pŏlonai′se (-z) n. **1.** Woman's dress consisting of bodice with skirt open over petticoat from waist downwards. **2.** (Music for or in style of) slow processional dance of Polish origin in triple time. [F, fem. (as n.) of *polonais* Polish f. med. L *Polonia* Poland]
polō′nium n. Radioactive metallic element forming the last stage before lead in the decay of radium. [F & med. L, f. med. L *Polonia* Poland (discoverer's native country) -IUM]
‖**polō′**... n. Sausage of partly cooked pork etc. [app. replacing *Bologna* or *Bolognian sausage*]
pō′ltergeist (-gist) n. Noisy mischievous ghost, esp. one manifesting itself by physical damage. [G (*poltern* create disturbance, *geist* GHOST)]
...′lt-foot n. (*pl.* -**feet**) & a. (arch.)... -foot... unkn.) + FOOT[1]]
pŏltrōō′n n. Spiritless coward; so ~ERY (4) n. [f. F *poltron* f. It. *poltrone* (perh. f. *poltro* sluggard); see -OON]
Pŏ′lў n. (*pl.*~**s**). (colloq.) Polytechnic. [abbr.]
pŏ′lў- *pref.* **1.** Many, much, as: ~**ade′lphous,** (Bot.) with stamens united in 3 or more bundles; ~**a′ndrous,** of or practising polyandry, (Bot.) ...ng numerous stamens; ~**andry,** polygamy ...h woman has more than one husband; ...consisting of many atoms, ...atoms or radicals; ...ore than two re- ...**aete** (-kēt) a. ...ē′t-) *adjs.*,

118

The Crisis Apparition

The soldier in the night

One kind of experience common to a great number of people is that of seeing the apparition of a friend or relative at the moment of that person's death. One such incident which was told to me when I was a child is a typical example.

During the Second World War my Uncle Jack, a corporal in the Royal Berkshire Regiment, was killed on the Anzio Beachhead during the Allied Invasion of North Italy.

On the night that he was killed, my mother woke up suddenly from a deep sleep convinced that her brother Jack had come into her bedroom. She sat upright in bed, fully awake, and to her utter astonishment saw Jack standing at the foot of the bed smiling at her.

In that split second my mother was filled with a feeling of joy and relief. 'Jack's all right,' she thought. 'He's come back safe and sound.' But immediately she realized that he could not possibly be home and, as this thought came into her mind, the figure of Jack vanished.

The whole experience lasted but an instant, yet my mother saw Jack with absolute clarity and detail.

'I knew then that he had been killed,' she said. 'But I didn't feel that I could tell anyone. Two days later we learned officially of Jack's death. He had been killed on the night that I saw him and at about the time when he appeared in my room.'

Despite the grief that she felt at his death, my mother always felt comforted by her experience that night. She felt sure that in that fraction of time Jack *was* actually there, and that at the moment of death his spirit had come to her for a last fleeting farewell.

'Jack and I were always very close,' she said. 'Although I realize that it was not his physical presence that I saw, nevertheless what I did see was real enough and had nothing to do with my imagination. I know that when I looked at him, and he smiled at me, a look of love and recognition passed between us.'

Many similar instances have been reported, especially during wars or at times of conflict, after people had seen loved ones who later were found to have been killed at the time of their appearance.

Because such apparitions are the result of an extreme emotion, usually during a crisis when a person is in grave peril or danger—at the moment of death, for instance—such apparitions are known as *crisis apparitions*.

The crisis apparition

Many people believe that a crisis apparition occurs when the mind of someone in difficulty or danger sends out a strong signal similar to the way that a television transmitter does.

The person who sees the image acts rather like a television set. The signal is somehow 'picked up' and seen by that person either as an apparition, or through an unexpected vision, or in a dream.

In whatever way such signals are received, they generally have one thing in common - they somehow communicate the feelings of the sender, leaving the receiver with the absolute certainty that something has happened and with a strong sense of dread or foreboding.

Not every crisis apparition is one which comes from a person at the moment of death. Some come as warnings, others as calls for help. The following stories, told in Daniel Farson's book Ghosts in Fact and Fiction illustrate this.

Steer to the north-east

Lord Halifax, a famous collector of ghost stories, was told of the case of a ship where the words 'Steer to the north-east' were found scrawled in the log in the captain's cabin. The captain had not written these words himself, and none of the crew admitted to it.

When the captain questioned his crew, his first mate said that he thought he had seen a strange man writing something in the captain's cabin.

On impulse, the captain altered course and headed north-east. Later in the day the look-out sighted a water-logged ship, and when the half-starved survivors were pulled aboard the first mate pointed to one of them exclaiming - 'That is the man I fancied I saw writing in the captain's cabin.'

The rescued sailor was asked to write the words 'Steer to the north-east' and when he had done so, his writing was found to be identical to the words in the log. He revealed that he had fallen into a trance the night before, and had declared afterwards that he was certain that rescue was near.

The Ghost from the Chicago Tugboat

Edmund Pacquet worked on a tugboat in the Chicago docks. One morning he 'appeared' in his sister's home, standing just behind her in the kitchen. His sister tells the story.

'This apparition stood with his back toward me, or rather partially so, and was in the act of falling forward - away from me - seemingly impelled by two loops of rope drawing against his legs. The vision lasted but a moment, disappearing over a low railing or bulwark, but was very distinct. I dropped the tea, clasped my hands to my face and exclaimed, "My God! Ed is drowned".'

Six hours earlier Edmund Pacquet had fallen overboard from the tugboat and drowned, in just the way she had seen.

Astral Projection

The case of Miss Tippett

Some friends of mine once lived in part of a house in North London, while the owner of the house, an elderly lady called Miss Tippett, lived in the rest of it.

Miss Tippett was a small brisk sort of person who believed in fresh air and exercise. So, she was always opening windows and hanging out clothes and bedding in the belief that everything should have a good airing.

As there was no central heating in the house, my friends did not share their landlady's liking for great draughts of cold air blowing into the house, and they went round shutting windows as fast as Miss Tippett flung them open.

One day the old lady suffered a stroke and had to be taken to hospital. As soon as the ambulance had left, my friends went into Miss Tippett's rooms, shut all her windows and doors, made her bed, and partially drew her curtains across to keep the sunlight from fading the covers and carpets.

Later they visited the hospital and found Miss Tippett completely unconscious. She had not moved, and she showed no reaction to anyone or anything, even though her eyes were wide open.

On their return home, my friends were astonished to discover that all the windows in Miss Tippett's part of the house were wide open. At first they thought someone must have gone into her rooms—a friend, perhaps. But they found all the doors still locked and there was no one to be seen.

Puzzled, they closed all the windows once more and made themselves a cup of coffee. While they were drinking it, they heard a series of bangs, thuds and crashes coming from Miss Tippett's bedroom.

Convinced that something was wrong, they approached the room rather hesitantly. Once again the windows were wide open, and now the bed-clothes had been flung back as if to air the bed. A number of Miss Tippett's jumpers were draped on the windowsill as someone might who was putting clothes out in the sun.

'It's Miss Tippett,' both my friends agreed. 'No wonder the doctors can't get through to her. She isn't at the hospital at all—she's here. Somehow she's here in this house.'

The old lady lay in her hospital bed for ten days.

During that time the house was racked with crashes and thumps as windows and doors flew open, and towels, tablecloths, clothes, and cushions were flung out of drawers and cupboards.

'It's as if the old lady is trying to do her spring cleaning,' my friends thought.

Perhaps they were right. One morning when they woke up the house somehow felt different. There were no more noises and nothing else was disturbed.

As for Miss Tippett, she had regained consciousness and was able to speak a little, though the stroke had left her without any movement in the right side of her body.

She never went back to the house, but spent the rest of her days in a comfortable nursing home.

What happened while she lay unconscious? 'Do you know,' she said. 'All the time I was lying there I dreamed I was at home doing my spring cleaning.'

Astral projection

Is it possible that Miss Tippett *was* in two places at once? And that while she lay in a hospital bed her life force—her spirit—separated from her body and was somehow projected back to her house?

Certainly Miss Tippett was a strong-minded and forceful woman. Was her determination to do something so strong that the power of her mind broke free from the limits of her body for a short time?

Many who study the paranormal suggest that it is possible for a person's immaterial self to separate from the body and project itself to another place. One name for this extraordinary theory is *astral projection*. The theory is that everyone has a spiritual double—a body that is free of its physical form and never dies. This is called the *astral body*.

While a person is alive the astral body and the physical body stay together. When a person dies, the astral body is freed from its physical counterpart. It is believed, however, that it is sometimes possible for the astral body to leave the physical body for a short time while the person is still alive.

Ghost Stories

I know someone who refuses to believe in ghosts because he has never seen one for himself. 'But what about all the thousands of people who *have* seen ghosts?' I once asked him.

'It's all imagination,' he replied. 'People just imagine things.'

Well, of course, people *do* imagine things, he's right about that. And what's more, some people can be susceptible to suggestion, so that if they are told about a ghost they are only too ready to believe it.

This happened in the famous case of the mad Vicar of Wapping when two men made up the story about a ghost and published it in a magazine. Despite the fact that the ghost was pure invention, it wasn't long before dozens of people claimed to have seen it for themselves, and one man even claimed to have been told about it by his grandfather.

Well, I have never seen a ghost, but I do believe in them because I have two very good friends who experienced one. My friends had seen their ghost long before I met them. But they only told me about it when I happened to ask them if *they* believed in ghosts.

When you read true accounts of ghosts and the supernatural, then you have to trust in what people say. You can't go round disbelieving in people just because you haven't seen a ghost for yourself.

What you can do, however, is to keep an open mind. This means that you should weigh up carefully what people say and decide for yourself whether you think they are being truthful, or imagining things, or exaggerating, or even lying.

If you have read the Ghost Dossier in this book you can see whether some of the theories suggested there apply to the particular story you are reading.

For example, it might be possible to apply the Energy Trace Theory to the story called 'The Coach of Death' on page 140. You won't find that the theories always fit perfectly. After all, Miss Selwyn was awakened by the sound of ghostly hooves, so how does *that* fit in with the theory?

The stories that are included in the following pages are there because they're good stories; so read them with an open mind, and, most important of all—enjoy them: that's what ghost stories are for!

The ghost of Marie Antoinette

One hot August day in 1901, two middle-aged women were visiting the Palace of Versailles just outside Paris. It was a stiflingly hot afternoon and the impressive state apartments were crowded with people.

'Why don't we leave the palace and walk to the Petit Trianon?' suggested one of the women, Miss Annie Moberly. Her friend, Miss Eleanor Jourdain agreed. The Petit Trianon is a little chateau that lies hidden from sight in the palace grounds. It was once the favourite retreat of Marie Antoinette.

A stroll to the tiny chateau seemed an attractive idea to both women. Perhaps there they would find somewhere cool and quiet to sit down and rest, away from all the tourists.

They set out in good spirits but after a

while both women fell silent. Somehow the mood of the afternoon had changed. Although a hazy heat still hung everywhere, Miss Moberly felt herself shiver. An unusual feeling passed over her. She felt that everything was unreal, as if she were walking in the scenery of a mirror or a picture.

The women walked on. Neither spoke. Yet both quickened their pace a little, hoping perhaps that by going faster they could walk away from the strange atmosphere of that part of the grounds.

It was with some relief that they spotted some people in the distance. Yet as the women drew nearer they became aware of something odd. The figures were dressed in the styles and fashions of over a hundred years before.

The women approached two men in long

green coats and three-cornered hats. 'Excuse me, messieurs, but we have lost our way,' faltered Miss Jourdain. 'Would you be kind enough to direct us to the Petit Trianon.'

The men were deep in conversation. They looked round at the two women in surprise. One of them answered abruptly, 'Walk straight on, Madame.' Then the men returned to their conversation.

The women hastened on. Soon they noticed a small cottage. Outside stood a woman and a young girl. Both wore eighteenth century dress and both stood unnaturally still as if frozen in time.

Miss Jourdain felt strangely disturbed. She knew she was not asleep, yet the figures seemed to be like those one might see in a dream. Still she and Miss Moberly did not speak and continued to walk in silence.

They now came to a point where the path branched left and right. As the women hesitated their gaze was drawn to a low-built wooden shelter overshadowed by trees. Both their hearts leaped.

Sitting on the steps was the most evil-looking man they had ever seen. His dark skin was deeply pitted and a large hat shaded his glowering eyes. One hand was grasping the front of a thick black cloak which he had drawn tightly round him.

The man stared at them with such brooding intensity that the women were

quite unable to move.

Suddenly they heard the sound of running footsteps. As if from nowhere a second man appeared, also in a cloak and hat. He called out to them in agitation, 'Don't go that way. Return to the house.' He looked back over his shoulder as if in fear of being pursued, and disappeared as mysteriously as he had arrived.

The astonished women took the path the man had indicated. They crossed a little rustic bridge and there beyond the trees they saw at last the Petit Trianon.

They made towards the house quickly, the image of the dark brooding man still in their minds. And it was then that they saw a beautiful woman sitting alone on the grass. She was wearing a long-waisted summer dress and a white scarf edged with green at her throat. She glanced up with such a cold haughty expression on her face that Miss Moberly and Miss Jourdain edged away from her and hurried past. They were thankful to have come at last to the house.

They went up the steps on to the terrace, where they saw a young man who took them round to the entrance. There they joined a party of tourists being shown over the apartments.

Having seen over the Petit Trianon they returned to Versailles for tea.

Neither lady commented on what they had seen until a week later. Then Miss Moberly suddenly asked: 'Eleanor, do you think that the Petit Trianon is haunted?'

Miss Jourdain had secretly given much thought to the subject. Now she said: 'Yes I do.'

They began to discuss the strange characters they had met that day. Only then did they realize that each had seen some people not noticed by the other—though they had never once been separated.

Excitedly they both resolved to each write down her own version of what happened. Then they would try to discover who the people they had seen actually were.

It was Miss Jourdain who first hit upon the idea that the haughty lady might have been Marie Antoinette. Friends in Paris told her that the ill-fated queen—who met her death at the guillotine during the French Revolution—was sometimes *seen* in the grounds of the Petit Trianon. And what was more, courtiers and servants who had attended her there were also *seen* too.

The day of the visit had been 10 August, the anniversary of the day on which an angry mob from Paris had first invaded the Palace and its grounds.

Further research uncovered another legend—that a messenger had been hurriedly sent to the Petit Trianon to warn Marie Antoinette of the approaching mob. Surely that was the running man they had seen.

As for the evil-looking man by the wooden shelter, surely he was none other than the Comte De Vaudreuil, a man who had been a member of the Queen's inner circle of friends but who had eventually betrayed her.

The two men in green coats could have been members of the special Swiss guard who always kept watch when the Queen was at the Petit Trianon. The woman and girl were possibly the wife and daughter of one of the royal gardeners.

On a second visit to Versailles in an attempt to retrace their original walk, Miss Jourdain discovered that the wooden shelter was no longer there. Nor was the little rustic bridge. Nor, indeed, was any other landmark they had seen. Yet old maps which she later studied showed that those landmarks *had* existed long ago.

Both she and Miss Moberly were now convinced that they had somehow been transported back through time to the Court of Versailles as it was in August 1789.

But were they? Many people believed that the two ladies had dreamed the whole thing, influenced by their sight-seeing tour of the palace.

Is there another explanation? Is there more than one dimension to time? Are the past, present, and future still here, but with the past and future hidden behind some secret veil which very occasionally some people are allowed to lift for a little while?

The haunted waxworks

In 1857 a man called Richard Turner decided to open a waxworks exhibition in Sacramento, USA. At that time hundreds of migrants had flooded into California after gold had been discovered at Sutter's mill in 1848.

In those days the famous waxworks of Madame Tussaud in London had been an enormous success and its fame had spread. Waxwork exhibitions had opened in some of the big cities in the USA. Turner was certain that the miners and people of Sacramento would be delighted if such a fashionable and popular form of entertainment could be set up for them to visit.

Accordingly, Turner travelled to London and managed to buy from the Tussaud family a group of waxworks which had not been popular in London. The group was that of six French characters awaiting execution at the guillotine during the French Revolution.

What particularly attracted Turner to these figures was that their faces had been made from moulds pressed from those of the actual victims after death. And the clothes were those taken from the victims' very bodies after the execution.

Turner made these the centrepiece of his exhibition and, just as he hoped, the tough, hard-bitten miners flocked to see it.

About a week after the exhibition opened, however, a strange thing began to happen. Every morning when the doors of the waxworks hall were unlocked, one of the figures from the guillotine group had moved to a new position and its head been removed from its body.

For some weeks, even though the hall was securely locked and a guard patrolled outside, by the next morning, the figure had always moved with the head taken off and placed, undamaged, on the floor.

Turner asked his caretaker to spend the night with him in the hall so that the mystery could be solved. Both men fell asleep and woke up to find that the figure had moved while they slept.

They tried again, and the second time they were more successful. Just before 2.30 in the morning the figure began to move. With mounting horror the men saw first an arm move, then the legs.

After a moment the stiff-looking wax face with its normally staring eyes seemed to come to life. Its features twisted into an angry frown and it said, in French: 'Is it not possible to get some peace at night? The people come to see us die. Now they come to see our spirits encased in wax. Come here no more during the hours of darkness or you will regret it.'

Turner and the caretaker did not wait in the hall to hear any more angry words from the ghostly figure in wax.

Sometime later, a young reporter from a Sacramento newspaper heard of the strange encounter and asked if he could stay in the hall with the waxworks to see for himself. At first Turner was unwilling, but finally he agreed and the young man was locked in the hall.

At exactly 2.31 the caretaker was aroused by screams and hammerings coming from inside. He quickly unlocked the door and the hysterical figure of the reporter slumped into his arms.

The reporter afterwards told his story.

He was, he said, convinced that the story of the sinister wax figure that came to life was just a tale made up by Richard Turner in the hope that more visitors would be attracted to the waxworks.

He felt sure that he would simply spend an uneventful night among a collection of wax dummies.

Yet as he sat in the eerie hall with its vaulted roof and dim wall lights, he began to grow less sure. The rows of figures were so uncannily like human beings that their complete stillness and the absolute silence made him feel nervous and uneasy.

He looked at the group of executed French men and women. There were five of them in all. They stood on individual stands, each with a neatly printed label at its feet.

There were two aristocrats, a man and a woman in faded silk and lace finery, a priest holding up his Bible, a young lady-in-waiting, and a man in a black suit with a frilled white cravat.

It was the man in the black suit who drew the reporter's attention, for it was about him that all the fuss had been made. It was this rather small figure that had previously come to life in the small hours of the night and from whose waxen face had come the whispered words: 'Come here no more during the hours of darkness or you will regret it.'

The man's name was Nicodème Léopold-Lépide. He had been a tax collector for a French duke. He had won the hatred of the poor with his greed and dishonesty.

Now, as the reporter stared at the figure, his nervousness increased. There was something about the stiff, waxen face that seemed somehow different to the faces of other effigies.

Was it the shadows, or did the face have an expression of sinister cunning?

The reporter gazed once more round the gloomy hall. Then, he looked again at the man in the black suit. What he saw made him frown. The figure was surely not standing quite like that when he had looked before.

He looked away again. When he looked back, the figure had changed its position once more. The reporter felt a chill creep over him. He stared at the figure and this time he saw it move. Slowly at first, then more quickly until, with a movement of its head, it stared straight at him.

Never had the young man seen a look of such evil and malice. A mist of terror clouded his eyes. And as he looked at the figure its head no longer seemed solid, but appeared ghostly and transparent.

Suddenly the figure stepped down from its stand and moved straight towards him. Backing hastily to the door, the reporter knocked on it urgently in order to call the caretaker.

There was no answer. The caretaker was asleep.

The young man banged harder as the wax figure moved closer. Then he turned and started to hammer with his fists on the door. As the horrid wax hands closed round his neck and the fingers pressed his throat, he screamed.

He remembered no more until he saw the friendly face of the caretaker bending over him anxiously.

As for the figure of M. Léopold-Lépide, it was found the next morning by the door, yet the head was on the floor next to the other figures.

When Richard Turner was replacing the waxwork on its stand he noticed that the fingers were flattened and out-of-shape. Could this have happened when they pressed against the reporter's neck?

In the end the waxwork was melted down and another figure was put in its place. After this there were no more strange movements and Turner's Waxwork Exhibition went on for the next twenty-five years.

The ghost who haunted a jet

Ghosts not only appear on land, and at sea; they have also been reported in the air, flying in aeroplanes. There are several stories of phantoms materializing in airports, and even a handful of accounts of ghost planes appearing in the localities where they crashed. But surely the most amazing story of all comes from America where the ghosts of a pilot and his flight engineer were said to have haunted a whole fleet of jets.

Of all the American ghost stories I have heard, this one of the phantoms that appeared in the jets of Eastern Airlines is certainly the most extraordinary. There are numerous eye-witnesses who have provided remarkable testimonies and the whole affair has been subjected to the most thorough investigation. But first let us look at the facts and go back to the very beginning of the affair . . .

The story started in 1973, when Eastern Airlines Flight 401—a L-1011 TriStar with 176 passengers and crew—was nearing Miami after a transcontinental journey from New York. The plane was in its approach over the swampy Florida Everglades when the pilot, Bob Loft, was told that his landing gear was not working.

While Captain Loft and his first officer began to check their controls to find where the fault lay, the flight engineer, Don Repo, climbed down into the jet's inspection bay to see if he could locate the trouble there. To facilitate their search, the jet was switched to automatic pilot, and the plane slowly circled the Everglades. When Don Repo reported back to his captain that the leading wheels were, in fact, down in the correct position, Bob Loft realized the fault probably lay in the indicator light which should have signalled that the landing procedure had been completed. He turned back to the instrument panel and began to remove the cover over the bulb. What the captain did not realize was that in swinging round—as a later enquiry discovered—he had accidentally switched off the automatic pilot.

So as he worked, he was not aware the

plane was now no longer under control and was rapidly losing height. It was only when the water and green vegetation of the swamp below suddenly hove into view that he realized what had happened. But tragically, it was too late to do anything. The TriStar plunged into the swamp, breaking up on impact. Only 77 of the people on board survived the terrible crash.

Strangely, the plane was not a complete write-off, and quite a number of expensive pieces of equipment, mainly from the kitchen galley area, were saved by the rescue teams. These were returned to Lockheed, the makers of the TriStar, to be reassembled in other TriStars.

And that was how, just three months after the crash, ghosts began to ride on Eastern Airlines. For on TriStar aircraft number 318, into which some of the salvaged parts had been put, the flight crew and cabin staff began to report the most eerie happenings.

On one flight, a vice-president of the airline got into conversation with a man who seemed strangely familiar. When he turned away the man disappeared—and then the official realized his fellow passenger had been Captain Loft.

During another flight between Miami and Atlanta, the engineer heard a loud knocking from the inspection compartment under the cockpit. He investigated and found it empty—but when he returned to his instrument panel he saw the face of Don Repo. The dead engineer was also seen by a group of caterers who were loading the same plane a few weeks later.

The crew of Flight 318 soon became convinced that if the ghosts of the two men were haunting their jet, their intenions were clearly benevolent and if they had any purpose it was to protect the aeroplane from a fate similar to their own. This theory was borne out when another TriStar was approaching Miami over the Florida Everglades. Before any member of the crew could turn on the public address system, the speakers crackled into life and an unidentified man's voice asked the passengers to fasten their seat belts.

In the weeks which followed, the ghosts

moved to other Eastern Airlines jets. A stewardess thought she saw smoke coming from a bulkhead wall in one TriStar and when she investigated, was confronted by the misty figure of Captain Loft. The cabin staff of another plane recognized one of their passengers as the dead captain, but when they challenged him the figure just vanished.

Even more extraordinary was the encounter of a flight engineer who went to check his instruments before take-off and found the ghost of Don Repo in his seat. The engineer said that the apparition spoke to him before disappearing and said, 'You don't have to check out the instruments, I've already done that.' And if any more confirmation was needed about the benevolent intentions of these phantoms, it came when Don Repo appeared to a further Eastern Airlines pilot and announced solemnly, 'There will never be another crash on an L-1101. We will not let it happen.'

Naturally, the story of the haunted airline attracted considerable interest, and the well-known investigative writer, John G. Fuller, travelled all over America, interviewing passengers and crew who had come into contact with the two ghosts. He admit-ted setting out on his inquiry thinking the whole story was probably a hoax, but the more evidence he gathered and the more people he spoke to, the more sure he was that this represented one of the most startling hauntings in American history. The results of his enquiry are published in a remarkable book, *The Ghost of Flight 401*.

The hauntings actually came to an abrupt end eighteen months after the original crash, when Flight 318 was exorcized by one of the officers who had become rather distressed by the incidents. He sprinkled water in the galley and recited some prayers. During the ceremony the man said he clearly saw the ghost of the dead engineer, Don Repo, one more time.

Today, the story of the ghosts who flew in TriStars is the subject of continuing debate. Some people remain convinced it never happened—it was all the result of over-imaginative minds. Others, especially those who were eyewitnesses to the events, are convinced that spirits have proved they can adapt their traditional roles even to the demands of the jet age.

For as one commented, 'If you believe that old houses and sailing ships can be haunted—then why not jet aeroplanes?'

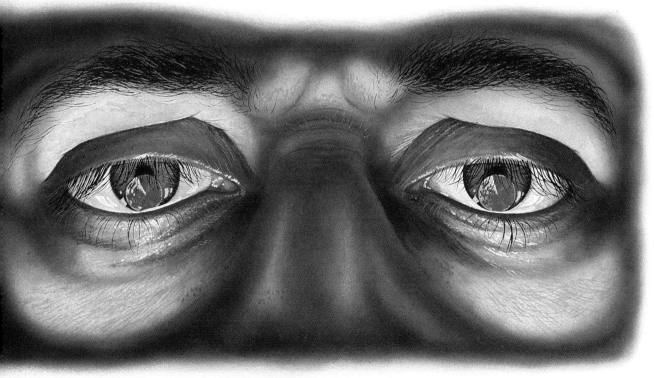

The curse of the Chases

The entrance slab was slowly drawn back from the tomb, and the men waited, terrified of what they might see. Daylight flooded into the gloomy vault. There was silence for a moment, then gasps of horror broke the stillness. Inside the tomb, there was chaos: the coffins had been hurled about once more. Even the heaviest coffin was upright against the wall. The curse of the Chases had struck again.

The place was Barbados in the West Indies, on a headland above the bay. There was, and still is, a church with a cemetery lying beside it. In the cemetery there is a strongly built stone tomb, the last resting-place of the Chase family.

The tomb is built of large stone blocks which are cemented together. A massive slab of blue marble once acted as a great, unmovable door on top of the entrance.

Only when another coffin was ready for the tomb was the door opened by a gang of strong men.

Yet between 1812 and 1820, someone or something opened the tombs. And inside, all the coffins were thrown violently about. Yet the door was untouched.

The vault was built in 1724 for the Hon. John Elliott, but there is no record that he was ever buried there. The first burial took place on 31 July 1807 when Mrs Thomasina Goddard was laid to rest. About a year later, the vault passed to new owners, the Chase family.

On 22 February 1808, the tomb was opened, so that the coffin of a small child, Mary Ann Chase, could be lodged there. The only other coffin inside was that of Mrs Goddard.

In those days mortality was high, especially among very small children. On 6 July, another young Chase was placed in the vault. The inside of the tomb was just as it was before.

But on 9 August 1812 the body of Thomas Chase was carried to the tomb. When the door was opened, the mourners were horrified to find that the coffins of the little Chase girls were both on end and upside down against one of the walls.

The coffins were replaced alongside Mrs Goddard's, and eight strong men put Thomas Chase's coffin on the floor. It was solid and made of lead. Then the stone-masons sealed up the vault once again.

On 22 September another member of the Chase family was brought to the vault, and the mourners had another shock. All the coffins, including the one made of lead, had been thrown about. On 17 November, exactly the same thing happened again.

By now the whole of Barbados knew the story, and the Chase family were becoming more and more desperate and upset. But no one could offer an explanation.

On 17 July 1819 another member of the family died. The Governor of Barbados, Lord Combermere, attended the funeral. When the vault was opened, he saw for himself that all the coffins, except Mrs Goddard's,

had again been hurled all over the tomb.

The Governor ordered that fine sand should be put down inside the vault to pick up the footsteps of any intruder. Then the tomb was sealed.

On 18 April 1820 the Governor ordered that the Rector should re-open the vault, even though no member of the Chase family had died.

This time the chaos inside was even worse than usual. One of the largest coffins had been flung against the door, which luckily opened outwards. All the sand inside was untouched except where the coffins had been thrown on to it. There were no footprints.

The islanders by this time were becoming more and more alarmed at these strange events. So the Governor decided to remove all the coffins and bury them in the earth in another corner of the churchyard. And there they remained in peace with no further trouble.

What possible explanations can be offered? No one believed that anyone had broken into the vault, even if it had been possible to move the heavy stone. It is also hard to imagine who would dare to break in, for superstition was rife on the island.

One writer claimed that Thomas Chase was a hard, cruel man who had many enemies in Barbados. He alleged that Thomas Chase had killed himself and that one of his daughters had starved herself to death. It was claimed that the other corpses had tried to expel her from the vault.

Others said that earthquakes had caused the upheavals. But how can earthquakes be confined to a few square metres of ground?

Another theory was that floods had caused the disturbances. But the tomb was at the very top of a headland. Besides, why were the remains of Mrs Goddard never disturbed?

The vault still lies in the churchyard in Barbados. But it remains empty, and the Chases lie buried peacefully in the earth.

The Stratford poltergeist

While the British Isles and Europe are sprinkled with haunted vicarages and rectories, few American churchmen have been harassed by noisy ghosts. But the unseen intruder that invaded the peaceful parsonage of the Reverend Eliakim Phelps in the sleepy town of Stratford, Connecticut, in 1850 ranks second to none as *the* classic American poltergeist.

A respected Presbyterian minister, Dr Phelps, lived in the parsonage for two years before anything strange started to happen. He had four children, of whom the youngest was a boy of three and the oldest a girl of sixteen. Admittedly, Dr Phelps was interested in occult matters and sometimes dabbled in amateur mesmerism and hypnosis. But he was in no way eccentric. The spiritualist craze was currently sweeping the country, and no one thought it queer when even a model churchman like Phelps occasionally held home seances and table-rapping experiments to try to contact the dead.

It was on a Sunday, 10 March 1850, that Dr Phelps's poltergeist troubles began. They would continue for the next eighteen months. That particular morning, Dr Phelps took his whole family with him to church. Their only servant, an Irish girl, was attending mass in nearby Bridgeport. Since the parsonage would be deserted for a few hours, Phelps locked it securely before leaving.

When he and his family returned, the front door was standing wide open. Dr Phelps thought this very peculiar, for the servant girl had not yet returned. When they went inside, a strange sight met the family's eyes. Chairs, tables, and other furniture were scattered about in wild disorder. Yet nothing had been stolen. In fact, a solid gold watch was lying exactly where it had been left that morning.

That afternoon, the Phelps family, as was their custom, went to church again.

However, Dr Phelps remained behind, in case their destructive visitor returned. He neither heard nor saw anything out of the ordinary all the time his family was gone. But when they returned and took up their normal activities in various parts of the house, they soon noticed that crockery and other objects were not in their normal places.

Strangest of all was what they found in the master bedroom. A sheet was spread over the bed, outside the counterpane. Underneath it was a nightgown with its arms folded across the breast and stockings placed where the wearer's legs would normally protrude. This crude effigy was laid out in the same fashion as a corpse usually was before it was placed in the coffin.

Next morning, the same sort of pranks continued—with a few new ones added. Furniture and other objects were seen to glide about. Phelps himself saw an umbrella, which was standing in the hall, suddenly rise up and fly across the room for twenty-five feet. A bucket, standing at the top of the parsonage stairs, came crashing down into the room below. Then smaller articles started to sail through the air. Nails, spoons, knives, dishes, forks, keys, bits of iron and tin were thrown about the house in all directions.

Later, the family again found evidence of some strange death-watch. A piece of black crêpe was discovered twisted about the knocker of the back door. The mirrors in the front rooms were draped with sheets and tablecloths, as was the custom in that part of the country when a dead person lay in a house shrouded for burial.

As these unnerving things continued in his home, Dr Phelps decided to call in a friend to confirm them. This man, also a clergyman, stayed for three weeks and became convinced that neither the servant girl nor any of the children were in any way responsible for the occurrences. Once, when a large raw potato fell out of nowhere next to Dr Phelps's plate, the two men experimented with it, dropping it from various heights to find out how high it must have fallen to make such a noise. They concluded that fifteen inches was right. But nobody could possibly have thrown it from that height without being detected.

A few days later, the two ministers saw a large chair rise from the floor and then bang down again. This happened with such violence that members of the family in other parts of the house could hear the whole parsonage shudder. The two dumbfounded clergymen also saw a heavy plated candlestick move from its customary place on the mantelpiece and swoop down onto the floor. There it beat itself continuously against the floor until it was shattered. On that same day, loud pounding noises were heard throughout the house, as if someone were striking the floor with an axe. Several times these sickening thuds were followed by frightful screams.

Day after day, these and other odd happenings plagued the Phelps family. Not surprisingly, word of them spread about the countryside and numbers of people came to see for themselves. Not one of them could account for the weird occurrences by any logical explanation. Yet they all agreed that neither the servant girl nor any of the

children could be producing them through trickery or practical jokes. Also, it was becoming more and more apparent that the strange goings-on were centred about two of the Phelps children—twelve-year-old Harry, and sometimes his sister Anna, who was four years older.

Once when Harry was out riding with Dr Phelps, twenty small stones were hurled at regular intervals into the carriage. Another time, Harry was tied up and suspended bodily in a tree. The boy was also caught up several times from the floor by some mysterious means and transported across the room. Once he was tossed into a cistern of rainwater. On still another occasion, Harry's pants were ripped to ribbons from the cuffs to the knees.

The longer the poltergeist activity went on at the Phelps house, the more destructive were its results. At one period, the poltergeist took to smashing windowpanes—no fewer than seventy-one of them. Dr Phelps himself witnessed the last one being broken by a flying tumbler that had sailed across the room. Harry was also present but standing a good twenty feet away.

Mysterious messages also began to appear. Often they were insultingly worded and signed with the names of neighbouring clergymen. While writing alone in his study one time, Dr Phelps paused for a minute and turned his back to the desk. When he resumed writing, he discovered that ten words had been written in large letters on the sheet before him. The message said: 'Very nice paper and very nice ink for the Devil.' The ink was still wet!

Young Harry continued to be the butt of most of the poltergeist's devilment. In one instance, his bed was set on fire. When eventually he was sent to school in far-off Philadelphia, the poltergeist pursued him even there. His books were ripped, his clothes were torn, and his very presence at the school caused such an uproar that he had to be sent home to Stratford. Strangely, when Harry was absent from the parsonage, comparative peace reigned in the house.

The most bizarre work done by the poltergeist occurred on 16 March, just a few days after its first appearance. Soon after breakfast on that day, Dr Phelps and some members of his family went into one of the little-used chambers of the parsonage. They were astounded to discover there eleven stuffed effigies—all of quite angelic beauty. All but one were female figures. Most were arranged in attitudes of prayer and devotion. They had been fashioned of clothing found about the house, stuffed to resemble human beings. A woman's dress would be filled with a fur muff, or pillows, or bunches of other dresses; shoes and bonnets were placed in appropriate places to complete the mysterious dummies. Before many of the figures lay open Bibles; gloves with pointing fingers indicated certain passages of Scripture. Some of the figures knelt by the beds; others bent their 'faces' toward the floor in attitudes of deep humility. But all were so arranged that they seemed to be worshipping the central figure of a dwarf, above which hung a flying form, possibly an angel.

One of these fantastic figures was formed from one of Mrs Phelps's dresses. As Dr Phelps gazed in awe at this strange sight, his three-year-old son entered the room. Seeing the kneeling figure, whom he assumed to be his mother, he whispered: 'Be still, everyone, Ma is saying her prayers.'

Many other queer things took place. One evening a 'vegetable growth' suddenly appeared on the living room carpet. It spread and seemed to take root; odd symbols appeared on the leaves for several minutes, after which it vanished. Heavy marble-topped tables would rise and crash to the floor. Spoons were bent double and thrown at the family. Turnips fell from the ceiling. The older daughter was frequently pinched. And, while the whole house was watched and doors were kept locked, the invisible sculptor continued creating his tableaux of lifelike effigies.

With the passing of the months, and the frequent absence of Harry and his sister, the 'Stratford Poltergeist', as it came to be known, ceased its malicious pranks, and at last the parsonage returned to its peaceful routine.

The intelligent and inquiring Dr Phelps, who kept many written accounts of the odd happenings, never could find out how they were produced. They were widely written up in the major newspapers and scientific journals of the day, and some of the occurrences were witnessed by news reporters. One of the most colourful figures then investigating psychic phenomena, Andrew Jackson Davis (known as 'the Poughkeepsie Seer'), came in person to inspect the Phelps house; he witnessed several occurrences. And Dr Phelps's own accounts of the disturbances were widely published; their straightforward style strongly indicates that he was perfectly honest in all that he reported. Indeed, Phelps would have had

little to gain by falsifying the accounts and stood to forfeit his good reputation had he done so.

In his later years, it was a still-baffled Phelps who wrote: 'I witnessed these occurrences hundreds and hundreds of times, and I know that in hundreds of instances they took place when there was no visible power by which the motion could have been produced.'

Today the old parsonage, now called the Phelps Mansion, still stands. Boarded up now, it can still be seen not far from the fashionable Shakespeare Theatre, for which the town is famous. As summer visitors watch *Hamlet* or *A Midsummer Night's Dream* in that theatre, few are aware that a stone's throw away there disported a classic American poltergeist whose antics once held the whole countryside in fear and awe.

The coach of death

Some years ago, a lady called Miss Selwyn, the headmistress of a girls' school in the south of England, was staying with friends who lived at Belgrade Castle in County Dublin, Southern Ireland.

Like many other buildings of its kind, Belgrade Castle has its share of ghosts, none of which Miss Selwyn knew about at the time of her visit.

It was during the summer, and Miss Selwyn was sleeping in a bedroom on the fourth floor. The room was bright and airy, and it looked out on to a beautiful sunken Italian garden on the southern side of the house. The garden was neatly laid out with paths and formal flowerbeds, and it was surrounded by marble balustrades and stonework.

Just beyond the Italian garden was an avenue of yew trees. Originally this avenue

had been part of the main driveway. It led from the road to the south side of the castle and then swept round the corner of the building to the front door.

Later this driveway had been closed, and the nearest trees had been removed to allow the sunken garden to be built. At the far end a ditch with one steep side had been dug to prevent cattle from wandering into the castle grounds. The new drive led directly to the front door across some fields.

One night Miss Selwyn went to bed as usual without any thought of ghosts and quickly went to sleep. Suddenly, in only a few moments it seemed to her, though in fact it was much longer, she woke in a state of great alarm. She did not at first know why. She lay quiet and still in the dark, her hair tingling on her scalp, her feelings on edge but her mind fully alert and wary,

wondering what could have awakened her.

Then suddenly she heard it! A loud and heavy sound of horses hooves clattering along the great Yew Avenue toward the house, accompanied by the constant jingling of harness and the deep rumble of heavy iron-tyred wheels.

A great coach was moving rapidly, the horses almost cantering along the avenue where no coach could possibly go.

Miss Selwyn had awakened in a state of alarm which must have come upon her while she was still asleep. Her alarm increased as she listened to the noise which seemed to rumble through the room, but it was several moments before she fully realized that there was no road outside and consequently nowhere where a heavy carriage and horses—or any kind of vehicle for that matter—could drive.

She suddenly realized that she was faced with some sort of ghostly manifestation. The noises seemed all the more eerie as she called to mind the setting of the old building and exotic garden. At this, she pulled the bedclothes over her head to shut out all sound—and any sight, too, if need be.

After a time, nothing more having happened, Miss Selwyn peeped out of her refuge to find, to her intense relief, that all was now silent and calm. The ghostly coach and four had passed on, leaving everything as quiet and peaceful as if they had never been, Yet Miss Selwyn found it hard to forget those dreadful sounds rumbling and crashing through the night. She lay still for some time, wondering if they would start again but all continued quiet, and eventually she fell asleep.

As soon as breakfast was over Miss Selwyn tackled her hostess about her terrifying experience during the night. The owner's wife, Mrs Richards, listened with polite interest but did not show the slightest concern. Then she explained in an almost casual way that the phantom coach was well-known and that every member of the family had heard it so often that they no longer minded it.

She and her husband had just forgotten to warn their guest about it. They told her not to mind it as nothing else ever happened in regard to it. Every now and again at regular intervals it was sure to be heard by someone.

The history of the manifestation as Miss Selwyn was able to piece it together is interesting, though distinctly grim.

It appears that some 150 to 200 years before, the owner of the castle was a judge. At that time the Yew Avenue was still part of the driveway which, running from the lodge gates, went sharply round the house to the front door.

Some disturbances had taken place in the town, and in the course of his duty the judge had tried one of the ringleaders, found him guilty and sentenced him to death. But the rest of the members of his group were still at large and thirsting for revenge.

They did not have to wait long, for shortly after the execution of their leader, they waylaid the judge as he drove late one evening from his club in the town back to his country estate. Men seized the horses and pulled the coachman off his box, while the footman at the rear was wounded by a shot and fell to the ground.

As for the judge, before he could defend himself, fierce bearded faces were thrust through the windows of the coach and he was shot and shot again until his dead body slumped across the seats.

Then the gang made off, and the horses, terrified by the tumult and the firing and with no hand to guide them, set off and galloped along the familiar road home. The lodge gates stood open and the horses continued in their frantic stampede, thundering along the avenue till at last they slowed and came to a stop, sweating and frightened, before the hall door.

The bewildered servants of the house went out to greet their master and saw the great coach standing there with no one in charge. Some ran to the horses' heads and others anxiously looked inside, straining their eyes in the darkness until they made out the blood-stained body of their master, on the seat of his coach, dead. What intense horror and distress must this tragedy have brought to his family and to his household! The old hall and the gardens around it echoed and re-echoed to the cries of his people as they mourned. No wonder then that the terrible event should impregnate the very stones and throughout the centuries re-enact itself, at least in part, for those who are sensitive enough to hear it.

This appears to be a case of a pure echo from the past, the repetition of an incident just as it occurred, without any variation whatsoever. It is strange that it should happen at odd times which are in no way connected with its anniversary, but as far as we logical human beings are concerned, these things are still shrouded in mystery.

Ghosts

When goblins hunt and devils roar
And witches meet on blasted heath
And bony hands knock on my door
You'll hear the chatter of my teeth.

When owls are hooting in the night
And ravens croak from leafless trees
And ghosts come howling gleaming white
You'll hear the knocking of my knees.

Of course, it's not that I'm afraid.
It's just the way my bones are made.

Eric Maple

394.2   Hunt, Roderick
HUN
        Ghosts, witches and
        things like that

$14.95

DATE			